Behaviour Management

Getting it right ✓

IN A WEEK

Susan Wallace

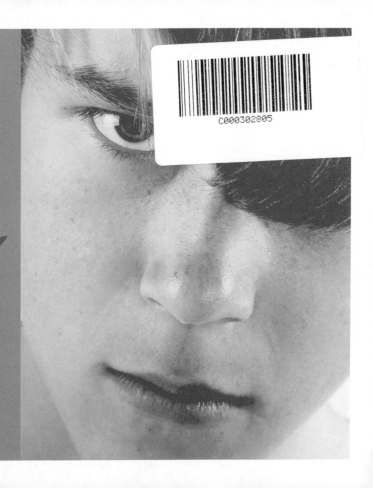

First published in 2017 by Critical Publishing Ltd

British Library Cataloguing in Publication Data

A CIP record for this book is available from the British Library

ISBN: 978-1-911106-26-5

This book is also available in the following e-book format:
MOBI: 978-1-911106-27-2

Cover and text design by Out of House Limited
Project Management by Out of House Publishing Solutions

Typeset by Out of House Publishing Solutions
Printed and bound in Great Britain by TJ International, Padstow

Critical Publishing
3 Connaught Road
St Albans
AL3 5RX

www.criticalpublishing.com

For orders and details of our bulk discounts please go to our website www.criticalpublishing.com or contact our distributor NBN International by telephoning 01752 202301 or emailing orders@nbninternational.com.

MIX
Paper from
responsible sources
FSC® C013056

CONTENTS

Susan Wallace

I am Emeritus Professor of Education at Nottingham Trent University where part of my role has been to support trainee teachers on initial and in-service teacher training courses. My own experience of classroom teaching has been mainly with 14- to 19-year-olds, and I have also worked in a local authority advisory role for this age group. My particular interest is in the motivation and behaviour management of reluctant and disengaged learners, and I've written a number of books and research papers on this topic. My work allows me the privilege of meeting, observing and listening to teachers from all sectors of education. It is to them that I owe many of the tips and ideas contained in these pages.

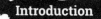

The teacher stands at the front of the room, calling the class to order. Most of the class pay attention, but a small group do not. They continue making a noise, shouting and laughing, tipping their chairs and avoiding the teacher's eye. The teacher claps her hands for quiet, but it has no effect. She raises her voice and calls for order. Members of the class who have been waiting quietly for the lesson to start begin to get restive. Now some of them are talking, too. The noise level is rising. Time is ticking. The teacher is wondering what to do next…

Does that sound familiar? Every teacher, no matter how experienced or confident they are, will come up against problem behaviour at some time or another. It comes with the job, and as a teacher you have a professional responsibility to deal with it. Experience and confidence help, of course; as does a supportive management team and an effective behaviour policy. And some teachers have it easier than others. But, across the profession as a whole, the problem of dealing with behavioural issues is one of the most common concerns voiced by teachers. This book is a response to that concern. It offers a straightforward toolkit of strategies and approaches, with examples of how they might be applied in practice. It is designed to be read and digested over just one week. It is short and to the point. It doesn't make you wade through a lot of theory, but it does point you to where you can find out more about the thinking and psychology behind the strategies on offer in case you want to know more – either out of interest or as part of a teaching qualification.

It is aimed at all teachers who would like to improve their behaviour management skills – either because they have a difficult class or because they know that, sooner or later, they'll meet one. It's designed to be useful, too, for teachers who may find themselves having to deal with just one or two disengaged or disruptive learners whose behaviour is spoiling things for the rest. Tom Bennett, chair of the Initial Teacher Training (ITT)

Behaviour Working Group, in his response to the 2015 Carter Review of ITT, refers to *the Three Rs of the Behaviour curriculum* (*Developing Behaviour Management Content for ITT*, July 2016). These three Rs, he suggests, are Routines, Responses, and Relationships. Routines are about establishing expectations and habits of behaviour; Responses are about implementing effective strategies and interventions; and Relationships are about developing our understanding of what drives our own behaviour and that of our learners. It is these same three Rs which underpin the content of each of the chapters that follow.

Most of the behaviour improvement strategies offered here are applicable across all age groups, 5 to 18; that is, from primary to secondary and further education. So, whichever sector you teach in, and whether you are a trainee teacher about to have your first experience of classroom practice or an experienced teacher looking for new ideas about how to handle that difficult class, there's plenty here for you.

What exactly is meant by 'disruptive' behaviour? Well, a useful definition to keep in mind is that it is behaviour which gets in the way of – or disrupts – learning, whether that is the learning of the whole class or only of those engaging in the behaviour. Ofsted has commented on the prevalence of *'low level disruption'* in today's classrooms: talking while the teacher is talking; not getting on with the task in hand; wandering about the room, and so on. This sort of behaviour poses an ongoing challenge to teachers at every stage of the education system. It can also be described as 'disengaged' behaviour, because these learners are choosing not to engage with their learning. An even greater challenge for the teacher is non-compliant behaviour – refusing to do, or avoiding doing, what is asked. And then, most serious of all, is behaviour which is actively confrontational. Whether the learner is 6 years old or 16, this can be a troubling experience for even the most confident teacher. But the more extreme behaviours are in most cases the least common. It is low level disruption which you are most likely to encounter, as the following figure illustrates.

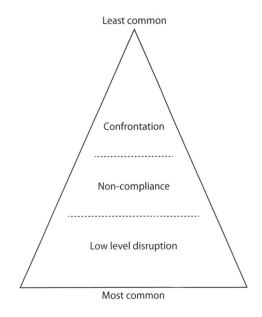

One of the key aims of the chapters that follow is to provide you with ways to prevent behaviour escalating up that triangle; to address it at the low level disruption stage so that it doesn't become openly confrontational.

This book is not about 'blaming' bad behaviour, however. It doesn't encourage labelling or demonising. Its emphasis is on building positive relationships as far as possible, and on looking for the causes of disruptive behaviour so as to be better able to address them. So, as well as offering plenty of tried and tested strategies and approaches for managing behaviour in the classroom, it also aims to give you some understanding of *why* learners might be behaving in the way they do. This is an important first step in learning not to take such behaviour personally because to do so would be to allow it to undermine your confidence in yourself as a teacher.

Because the book is written for teachers of all age groups, it uses the term 'learner' rather than the more specific 'pupil' or 'student'. 'Learner' also serves to remind us of *why* behaviour management is so important. It's not just about making life more peaceful for the you and the rest of the class. It's about supporting and connecting with children or young adults who have disengaged from the learning process and about getting them back on track; keeping open the opportunity for them to achieve and flourish; encouraging them to think of themselves as *learners*.

The book is divided into seven main chapters designed to be read over the course of a week, one chapter each day. Each chapter sets out a number of strategies for you to try. Many of these are divided into two or more sub-strategies so that you can experiment and see what works best for you and your class. Following each strategy is a scenario showing how it might look when put into practice, or suggesting ways you might audit your own teaching to judge how it could be incorporated. Ideas or theories which underpin or support the wider strategies are briefly summarised under the heading, 'A Spot of Theory'. There are several of these in each chapter. This feature, together with the Further Reading listed at the end of the book, is provided in case you wish to learn more about the relevant theoretical background, or might want to reference it in your studies.

The seven daily chapters follow a logical progression. **Day 1** provides a range of strategies for emergency use. They are techniques that can be applied straight away, should you need them, so as to buy yourself some breathing space for **Day 2**, in which the focus is on diagnosing what's going wrong and why. **Day 3** offers ways in which to avoid disengaged or low level disruptive behaviour escalating into anything worse, while **Day 4** goes on to suggest some effective strategies for dealing with noise. The problems of boredom and disengagement are tackled directly on **Day 5**; and then **Day 6** presents strategies for dealing with ringleaders, cliques and attention seekers. The final day, **Day 7**, sets out some useful techniques for managing your own natural fears and anxieties – those that arise when facing, and having to deal with, problem behaviour.

If you are very short of time, you'll find towards the end of each chapter just one suggested strategy out of the many outlined, presented under the heading, *If you only try one thing from this chapter, try this*. And finally, each chapter closes with a checklist which enables you to note down what worked best for you, and with whom.

This book is designed to be easily read, easy to use, and easy to relate to your own practice and experience. Some of the scenarios may alarm or amuse you; others may feel all too familiar. Its ultimate purpose is to help you to manage classroom behaviour more confidently and effectively, and to support you in building a positive and productive classroom environment where the focus can be more firmly on the enjoyment and rewards of learning and teaching.

DAY 1: Firefighting: strategies for emergency use

An emergency toolkit

In this first chapter you'll find some ideas and tips for behaviour management which you can put into practice immediately, buying yourself time to read and plan for some of the strategies you'll find in later chapters. Sometimes, coping with a difficult class or a small group of disruptive learners can feel like fighting a fire. You no sooner have one thing under control than something else flares up to challenge you. Here you'll find some simple approaches that many teachers have found work well. Some of them, such as the use of *Praise* and *Body Language*, will be revisited in various ways in later chapters because they are absolutely essential to your behaviour management toolkit.

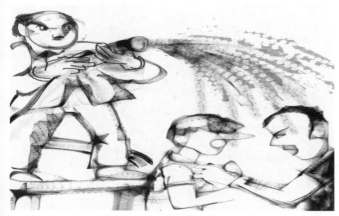

Classroom firefighting 101

Today's strategies

● Body language:
   1. Cool and confident
   2. Getting out there
   3. Happiness

● Using positive language:
   4. Tell it like it is
   5. Question marks
   6. Respect

● The three-step settle:
   7. Ready (tell, don't ask or answer)
   8. Steady (running commentary)
   9. Go (a clean start)

● Praise and preparation:
   10. Plan B
   11. Accentuate the positive
   12. Be prepared

Strategy: Body language

The way you stand, move and act communicates a lot about the way you feel. You may be trying to tell the class that you're in charge, but if you're standing there rooted to the spot with your shoulders hunched and your arms folded, your body language is telling them that you don't feel at all confident or comfortable and that, in fact, you feel very far from being in charge. Body language is something that we 'read' without even thinking about it. Learners – whatever their age – will pick up on your body language quite unconsciously, just as you'll pick up on theirs. (Imagine, for example, walking into a classroom and finding that all the learners are staring at the floor with their arms folded.) If your mannerisms and behaviour are confident and self-assured – even if at first you have to pretend and 'act' it – that is what the class will see: a teacher who is in control. And as the class respond to you, this positive feedback will begin to build your confidence for real.

1. Cool and confident

Let the learners see you enter the classroom with a bounce in your step. Make plenty of eye contact (but don't overdo it; that could look scary!). Stand up straight. Try to avoid crossing your arms – that's a defensive stance. If you're feeling nervous, don't attempt to pick up and consult a sheet of paper or read anything out from one, because any slight tremor will rattle the paper and give you away. Use a tablet or even small sheets of card instead for your lesson plan or lesson notes.

2. Getting out there

Don't talk to the class from behind your desk or table. Looking as though you need a barrier between yourself and the class can send a message that you're nervous or uncomfortable about being with them. Get out there and walk about. Don't lurk nervously in the 'teacher's space' at the front of the class. Move about the room as much as is practical. This sends out the message that the classroom is your territory – you're in charge.

3. Happiness

Look pleased to be there. Okay, you may not be – but act as though you are. Smile. Look and act enthusiastic – about the subject, the topic, the class, the weather – anything. Cheerfulness can be infectious. And it models the attitude you want to see in your learners.

Positive body language	Negative body language
Teacher smiles, looks cheerful	Teacher looks miserable, cross, anxious
Teacher moves confidently about the room	Teacher is static, occupies minimum space
Teacher uses hand gestures for emphasis	Teacher folds arms or keeps arms by side
Teacher makes eye contact with as many learners as possible while talking or listening	Teacher avoids eye contact, keeps gaze on back of room or whiteboard etc.
Teacher puts no barriers between self and class	Teacher stays behind table or desk
Teacher walks, talks, gestures with energy	Teacher's movement and talk lack energy
Teacher demonstrates keen enthusiasm for the topic (think Brian Cox!)	Teacher appears bored, uninterested, unenthusiastic (think about your own most boring teacher!)

Strategy: Using positive language

When you find it necessary to tackle learners about their behaviour, there are some strategies which will make your intervention more likely to succeed. The key here is to avoid escalating the situation. Non-compliance can quickly turn to open confrontation if it is not handled in the right way. These three strategies will help you to address behaviour issues positively, calmly and briefly, without turning them into a long-running drama that could end up disrupting learning for the individual or the whole class.

4. Tell it like it is

Rather than phrase your intervention/correction as a negative command (for example, *'Jonah, stop swinging on your chair'*), phrase it as a statement of fact, drawing the learner's attention to their disengaged or disruptive behaviour and signalling that you have seen it and want it to stop (for example, *'Jonah, you are swinging on your chair. We have a class rule about that'*). This approach has the advantage of letting the rest of the class know that you can see what's going on and have asserted control, without the disadvantage of creating a confrontation by issuing a direct order.

5. Question marks

Alternatively, you can phrase your intervention/correction as a question aimed at drawing the learner's attention to their behaviour and raising awareness of rules of behaviour for the class as a whole. For example: *'Jonah, what is our rule about sitting safely?'* Or *'Jason, how should we sit on our chairs?'* Or *'Jason, what did we agree when we discussed safety rules in the classroom?'* The Question Marks approach keeps the intervention positive, brief and low-key.

6. Respect

When making an intervention it's important to model the attitude of respect you want to see in your learners. This means not shouting or using an unnecessarily loud voice; explaining consequences but not issuing threats; not displaying anger or losing your temper; remaining civil and never displaying dislike for a learner or learners, however we may feel about them.

A Spot of Theory

Bill Rogers, in his book, Cracking the Hard Class *(Paul Chapman Publishing, 2006), stresses the importance of using* positive corrective language *when intervening to correct a learner's behaviour, and urges us to* 'keep the fundamental respect intact' *(p 93).*

Compare the way these two teachers intervene to correct behaviour in their class. Judging from their approach, which teacher do you think sounds more calm and in control of the situation?

Teacher A uses positive language	Teacher B uses negative language
'You're interrupting me, Eliot. What's our rule about listening in this classroom? That's right. Thank you.'	'Eliot, be quiet. I said be quiet! I'm talking. You don't talk while I'm talking. Now be quiet and listen. I said be quiet!'
'Alia, you're wandering about. What did we agree when we talked about this? Yes. Good.'	'Alia, sit down. I've told you before, you're not allowed to wander about. Sit down now! I said now! Sit down or there'll be trouble.'
'Lilli, you're staring out of the window again. If you don't get on with your work, you won't get it finished on time.'	'Lilli, what are you doing? Why aren't you getting on with your work? Why are you staring out of the window. Get on!'
'Alia, you're out of your seat again. What did we just agree about this?'	'Sit down, Alia. Is there something wrong with your ears? Why don't you just listen to what I'm telling you? Why are you wandering about? Don't you listen to anything I say?'

Question: Teacher B does ask questions – but they aren't the sort of questions we need to use for the Question Marks strategy. Why are the following negative rather than positive questions?

 'Why don't you just listen to what I'm telling you?'

 'Why are you wandering about?'

 'Don't you listen to anything I say?'

Answer

☑ All these are 'open' questions. In other words, they don't necessarily encourage the learner to think constructively about their behaviour, and the response may be negative or aggressive. This means there's a risk the response may be rude, negative, challenging or confrontational. *(Q: 'Why are you wandering about?' A: 'Because I'm bored / because this lesson is boring / because I want to / because you can't stop me'.)* 'Why' questions are less useful in this context than 'What' or 'How' questions.

Strategy: The three-step settle

This is a three-stage strategy which generally works well at the beginning of a lesson to settle a noisy or disruptive class. It works by marking out for the learners a clear boundary between informal, social time and formal class time where the focus must be on learning. It helps you avoid 'messy' starts and the frustration of repeated calls for quiet. It becomes increasingly effective through repetition, as learners come to recognize the three stages to settling down ready to learn. You'll find additional strategies for ensuring an orderly start to the lesson later in the book. But this is a good one to kick off with.

7. Ready (tell, don't ask or answer)

Begin by *telling* the learners what you want them to do. This should take the form of clear and briefly stated instructions *('Sit down quietly.' 'Everyone looking this way. Thank you.' 'Everyone put on their listening ears now.')* It's important that you tell rather than ask. *Telling* the learners what to do sends the signal that you are in charge. If you phrase your instructions as questions it doesn't have the same effect *('Will you sit down?' 'Can you please be quiet?' 'How long am I going to have to wait?' 'How many times do I have to tell you?')*. You also need to avoid getting into conversation or answering questions at this stage. Tell learners you will talk to them/ answer their question as soon as the class is settled and ready to work.

8. Steady (running commentary)

While the class is responding to what you're telling them to do, you should deal with disruption or distraction by describing what you see, using the positive sort of language we've just looked at in *Tell it like it is*. *('Daniel and Ruby, you're still chattering.' 'Ramesh, what did we agree about playing with pencils?' 'Josh, you haven't sat down yet.')* At the same time, you may need to continue the *Ready* stage, telling and reminding the class to settle.

9. Go (a clean start)

Once you have the learners sufficiently settled – *but not before* – you should greet them as a class. *('Thank you. Good morning, everybody. Good to see you all. How is everyone today?'* etc.) This is the signal that learning time has started. The time for chatting or messing about is over. You have drawn a clear line. You've established a clean start to your lesson rather than having to struggle with a 'messy' one. You can now introduce the lesson/topic/activity.

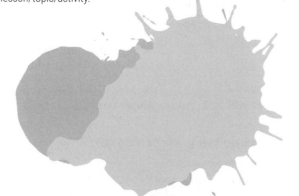

Here is a teacher using the Three-Step Settle. See if you can identify the steps. Notice particularly:

1. how she combines steps 1 (Ready: tell, don't ask or answer) and 2 (Steady: running commentary);

2. how this strategy establishes positive interaction with the class (no shouting, no criticism, no 'telling off') from the outset. The class begins in a co-operative way rather than starting off as a battle.

> " *Walk in quietly. Sit down now. Thank you. All eyes this way. Listening ears on.*
>
> *Sit down now Ryan; I'll answer that question in a minute when you're all settled. All eyes this way now.*
>
> *Thank you, Ira. We'll talk about that in a minute when you've settled. Everyone sitting down now.*
>
> *Hanya, you're wandering about. It's settling down time now. Listening ears on, everybody.*
>
> *Neel you're still talking. All eyes this way, please. Thank you.*
>
> *Well now, good morning everybody. I hope you're all ready to show me how hard you can work this morning...*

A Spot of Theory

Bill Rogers, in his book, Classroom Behaviour *(4th edition, Sage, 2015), suggests that settling a class by means of these three steps should take place during the first three minutes of the learners entering the classroom. This is a good target time to aim for. You may find with practice that you achieve it in an even shorter time as your class becomes accustomed to settling down in this way.*

Strategy: Praise and preparation

A lot of classroom behaviour difficulties can be forestalled and prevented by careful forward preparation and planning. You'll see this same advice cropping up in various contexts in the chapters that follow. Sometimes you can predict who's going to cause trouble and how, and can take measures in your lesson plan to forestall this. But a lot of minor, everyday classroom incidents and behaviours happen randomly, and yet are easy to prevent from escalating with a little preparation. Praise, too, is one of your most powerful tools. Learners who have come to think of themselves as 'naughty' or as troublemakers may come to class intending to live up to that role and expecting all their interactions with the teacher to be negative ones. Accentuate the Positive explains how you can break that pattern and bring about a real improvement in behaviour.

10. Plan B

Always have a Plan B.

* If the lesson you've planned is failing to engage the learners, a different approach such as a change of teaching/learning strategy may re-engage their interest.

* If the class, or some of them, complete their work more quickly than you thought they would, they may grow bored and disruptive. Always have an extension activity up your sleeve.

* Is there a learner or group of learners who refuse to join in with an activity (they've 'done it before'; they get nervous doing the activity; they're afraid of looking silly; they 'don't understand' why they've got to do it)? Have an alternative task or activity you can set them which will achieve the same learning outcomes.

* Technology suddenly lets you down? Don't spend ages fiddling with the data projector/interactive whiteboard or whatever. The class will grow bored and will disengage. It could be difficult to get their attention back. So don't be afraid to abandon Plan A and use a low-tech Plan B alternative instead.

11. Accentuate the positive

Are there learners in your class who are habitually in trouble, always coming in for criticism or correction? Try this experiment. Look carefully for something in their behaviour to praise. It's usually possible to find something. (*'Thank you for holding the door open, Harry.' 'Well done for remembering to put the book away, Sheena.' 'Thank you for helping Wajeed find a pencil, Lilli.' 'You're looking very smart and keen this morning, Mo.'*) Make a point of suspending criticism and offering praise instead at any opportunity you can find. Praise is a very powerful reward. It can help learners who have got used to grabbing attention by misbehaving to discover that they can get attention instead for positive behaviour. This is one of the ways in which the application of behaviourist theory – encouraging the behaviour we want by rewarding it – can be very useful to busy teachers.

12. Be prepared

'I can't do it because I've left my [whatever it is] at home.' If you teach older children or young adults, you'll be familiar with this avoidance tactic.

They've come without their pencil/pen/ruler/geometry set/calculator? Always have some spares. They've lost the handout or worksheet you gave them? Always have some spares. These apparently small hitches have the potential to hold up the flow of the lesson, giving learners an opportunity to disengage and 'mess about' or grow bored while you try to sort things out. You know it's going to happen, so always come prepared.

In the following scenarios, what steps could the teachers have taken to avoid the situation becoming a problem?

- The teacher has planned for a task to take 20 minutes. After 10 minutes learners begin to raise their hands to say they've finished. The teacher can't get around them all. They grow bored and noisy.

- Anton is being a nuisance as usual. The teacher is getting increasingly cross and keeps telling him to sit down and be quiet. Although he's not getting on with his own work, Anton keeps leaning across and helping his neighbour with the task. The teacher says, *'Anton! What are you doing? Stop interfering! Get on with your own work!'*

- The data projector won't work. The teacher is frustrated because there's a lot of information to get across in today's lesson and getting it all up on slides seemed like a good way of doing it. So the teacher perseveres, fiddling about with the computer while the class gets noisier and noisier.

Finished Miss!

Checklist

Use this to keep a record
of what worked well for
you and what didn't.
A strategy that works with
one class may not work so
well with another. Keeping
a checklist helps you to
work out what factors or
learner characteristics call
for one approach rather
than another. There's a
line at the bottom for you
to add your own most
frequently used strategy, if
it's not already included in
the list.

Strategy	Tried it with...	On...(date)	It worked	It didn't work	Worth trying again?
1. Cool and confident					
2. Getting out there					
3. Happiness					
4. Tell it like it is					
5. Question marks					
6. Respect					
7–9. The three-step settle*					
10. Plan B					
11. Accentuate the positive					
12. Be prepared					
Your own strategy?					

DAY 2: Troubleshooting

Ways to work out what's going wrong and why

Today's chapter is slightly different from the rest. It's about diagnosis. It encourages you to ask yourself the question: *Why* is this learner behaving like this? When you've worked out the likely answer, you'll find some suggested strategies and approaches for addressing that particular problem. Of course, it's not always easy to see what the problem is. But the more approachable you are – the more you focus on seeing your learners as individuals – the more likely you will be to understand what's getting in the way of their learning.

Troubleshooting

These strategies cover what to do if it seems that the learner:

- is finding the task too easy:
    1. Easy peasy
    2. Expert-ease
    3. Diversify

- is finding the task too difficult:
    4. Getting to know you
    5. Step back
    6. Vive la difference

- sees you as the 'baddie':
    7. Nothing personal
    8. Breaking the cycle

- feels afraid of looking 'stupid':
    9. Safety in numbers
    10. No pouncing

- assumes they can't do the task:
    11. Yes we can!
    12. Small steps

- would rather be somewhere else:
    13. Where do we start?
    14. Take a break

- thinks *you'd* rather be somewhere else:
    15. When you're smiling
    16. Cheerleading

Strategy: If the learner is finding the task too easy

There will inevitably be a range of abilities and previous knowledge in any class. Hitting the right level for all learners is difficult, and some may become bored or tune out because it's too simple for them or they've heard it all before. A bored learner is potentially a disruptive learner, so it's wise to plan ahead to avoid this problem.

1. Easy peasy

When planning your lesson, make sure you include some *extension activities* for those learners who are able to complete the work more quickly than the rest of the class or who may have covered it already and are able to skip it altogether. Extension activities should be designed to provide sufficient challenge to keep the learner's interest, but not be so challenging as to make them lose heart and give up. Otherwise you're back where you started! To get it right you'll need to do a careful assessment of learners' current state of knowledge and skills.

2. Expert-ease

Peer mentoring is a useful and very positive way of harnessing the energy and knowledge of learners who are finding a topic or task too easy. Partner them with a learner or learners who are finding it difficult or who need additional help and encouragement. This can build the confidence of both sets of learners: the 'experts' see that their expertise is being acknowledged and rewarded, while those they are 'mentoring' feel supported and are helped towards a sense of achievement.

3. Diversify

If you are already aware of which learners may need a more challenging task or activity to keep their interest, you can try dividing the class into several groups, each working on a slightly different task, one of which is the more challenging. However, it's important here to have several groups, not just two, because this would be seen by the learners as the 'best' group and 'not the best' group – which would be divisive and counterproductive, and could prove disheartening for those who are already finding learning difficult.

Which of the following do you think would qualify as a constructive and effective extension activity?

A. If a learner finishes a task before everyone else, give them more of the same to do.

B. If several learners finish ahead of the rest of the class, tell them to do some quiet reading.

C. If anyone finishes ahead of the allotted time, they're allowed to do some work on their ongoing project.

D. Learners who complete the task quickly are given a slightly more difficult or complex version of the task to work on.

E. If anyone claims to have 'done this before' or says the work is 'too easy', tell them to do it anyway because it's good practice for them.

F. Learners who claim the task is too easy for them are asked to use their existing knowledge to design some questions for the rest of the class.

Answer

 D and F would be useful extension activities.

Strategy: If the learner is finding the task too difficult

This can be a major reason for disruption in the classroom. If learners are finding – or fear they will find – the work too difficult for them, they'll do almost anything to avoid doing it. The fear of failure or humiliation is a very powerful factor here. And so it's essential to avoid backing learners into a defensive position where they'll misbehave just to avoid doing the work.

4. Getting to know you

With any class of learners it's important that you get a clear idea, as quickly as possible, of each individual's starting point in terms of their skills, knowledge and understanding. Only then will you be confident of pitching tasks at the right level. Getting learners to talk about themselves is a good starting point. Try this: working in pairs, learners have five minutes each to tell their partner about themselves – their interests, likes, dislikes, what they're good at and what they feel they're not so good at. Each then uses the information to 'introduce' their partner to the rest of the class. This can be presented as *The TV Interview Game*. Learners enjoy it and it should give you a lot of helpful information.

5. Step back

If it's clear that a learner or group of learners are finding a task or an explanation too difficult and are in danger of disengaging, take them a step or two back – right back to basics, if necessary. We can't build on our learning unless the foundations are secure. If someone hasn't understood fractions, for example, it's no good expecting them to be able to tackle quadratic equations. If they can't recite the alphabet, they won't be able to use a dictionary. Sometimes it will be necessary to take many steps back until you find the point at which the learner can begin to engage and move forward. This may call for you to spend some time working one-to-one or with a small group. So what happens with the rest of the class? That's where the next activity comes in useful...

6. Vive la difference

Planning for differentiated tasks and activities can give you the flexibility to work with individuals and small groups while the rest of the class is usefully engaged in learning at a level which is appropriate to them. This is useful to you in a number of ways. It allows you the opportunity to get to know learners and their individual learning needs; it gives you space to provide additional support to individuals who need it; and it provides a structure in which learners who need a greater challenge can be set tasks that keep their interest and stretch them.

Strategy in action

Read the following two scenarios and decide in each case which of the three approaches (Getting to Know You, Step Back and Vive la Difference) the teacher should use.

Which do you think would prove most useful?

Should they try more than one, and – if so – why?

- The teacher is explaining something to the class as a whole. She notices that several learners – three in all – are looking puzzled or bored. They are fidgeting around in their chairs and are clearly not paying attention to what she's saying. What would you advise her to do?

- The teacher is meeting the class for the first time. He has heard that some of the learners are 'difficult' and can be disruptive. He spends some time planning his first lesson with them. Which of the three approaches would you advise him to consider? (You may choose more than one.) How would you explain to him the reasons for your suggestion?

Getting to know you: "This is Damien. He likes girls. Girls like hime...and it's not fair!"

Strategy: If the learner sees you as the 'baddie'

Learners who have previous negative experience of school or of authority figures such as parents or carers, and who have often been in trouble or struggled with learning, are likely to see teachers as their enemy, as someone who may at any moment scold or humiliate them. This creates a serious barrier to their learning; and treating you as though you are the enemy will probably involve them in behaviour that is disruptive and confrontational. If this is the case, you have two courses of action and you will need to use both of them. They are: Nothing Personal and Breaking the Cycle.

7. Nothing personal

Always keep in mind that the learner's attitude is unlikely to be based on a personal dislike of you. You – as the teacher – are just a convenient target for their resentment of all and any authority figures who have caused them unhappiness in the past. If you take their behaviour personally you will be drawn into conflict, and this will only reinforce the learner's belief that teachers are the enemy. If you can avoid taking disruptive or confrontational behaviour personally, you will also be able to avoid reacting in a negative way and perpetuating the problem. It will allow you to respond instead in an appropriate way to defuse the conflict.

8. Breaking the cycle

If a learner's previous experience has taught them to treat the teacher as an enemy, the solution is to break this cycle by demonstrating that a teacher can be supportive, good-humoured and positive. This, of course, moves the spotlight from the learner's behaviour to your own. If you want learners to behave appropriately and with respect, you have to model that behaviour yourself. This isn't always easy in the face of disruption or non-compliance; but it is, nevertheless, essential. A teacher who flares up with anger, loses their temper, uses insults or shouts aggressively can't expect learners to behave any better. Breaking the cycle calls for a great deal of patience and self-control, but the pay-off is worth it.

Here are five effective ways in which you can put these strategies into immediate action.

1. If you show disapproval, always make it clear that it's the learner's behaviour you disapprove of, not the learner themselves.

2. Make sure your own behaviour always provides the best possible role model for the behaviour you expect from your learners.

3. Always be approachable. Listen to your learners; don't just talk at them.

4. Interact with your learners by name, individually, whenever you can.

5. Always make sure that your positive interactions (eg praise, smiling, greeting) with any one learner outnumber your negative ones (eg reprimanding, correcting).

A Spot of Theory

Paul Dix, in his book, Taking Care of Behaviour *(Pearson/Longman, 2009), reminds us that monitoring our own behaviour as teachers is an essential first step to improving the behaviour of our learners. He describes the teacher whose temper flares suddenly from 0 to 60, and points out the negative impact this would have on a class, both in terms of setting a bad example and in terms of making the classroom an unpleasant and frightening place to be.*

Strategy: If the learner feels afraid of looking 'stupid'

Learners may disengage from what's going on in the classroom if they're scared of making a fool of themselves by exposing their lack of understanding or skill. Or perhaps they feel anxious about speaking up for other reasons: the possibility of being mocked by their peer group, for example. Once they've opted out, there is the danger that their behaviour will distract or disrupt the class. So here are a couple of ways to draw these learners in.

9. Safety in numbers

Some learners may be prepared to do almost anything to avoid speaking up or attempting an activity in front of a class full of their peers. But they will feel much less exposed if they are part of a small group, particularly if the answer, task or outcome can then be presented as a group effort. This allows anonymity for the individual learner. Incorporating small group work into lessons (although it can cause complications in terms of individual assessment) is a very effective way of drawing in learners who 'opt out' of whole-class learning.

10. No pouncing

When you are asking the class questions, it's important to remember that this can feel very threatening to learners who fear you may pick on them and expose their inability to answer correctly. They may view this as a threat of ridicule, and so they'll take evasive action in the form of disruptive behaviour. So, rather than 'pounce' on learners by name when asking questions, you could try:

* Hands up – asking for volunteers to answer. But this can lead to the same few learners answering all of the questions. So you could also try:

* Silent voting (for closed questions). Learners write their response on their mini-whiteboard or a sheet of paper and hold it up so that you can see who's got it right.

* Dividing the class into teams for question time – teams answer collectively.

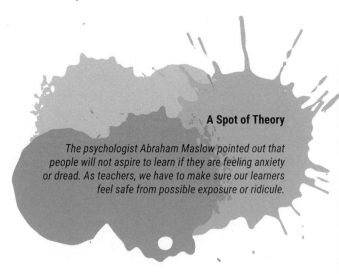

A Spot of Theory

The psychologist Abraham Maslow pointed out that people will not aspire to learn if they are feeling anxiety or dread. As teachers, we have to make sure our learners feel safe from possible exposure or ridicule.

How do you recognise when the reason a learner is opting out or being disruptive is because they're desperate to avoid appearing stupid?

The following scenario demonstrates some of the tell-tale signs.

✸ If you can see them, why do you think the teacher, in this case, can't?

❝ *Okay. Settle down. Let's see how much you can remember about what we did yesterday.*

The teacher points.

❝ *Gautam! What were we talking about yesterday?*

Gautam answers correctly, looks relieved and pleased, and the teacher moves on.

❝ *Now, how do we work these out?*

He looks along the tables of learners and then pounces.

❝ *Brianna! Why don't you tell us? Brianna? You won't find the answer by looking out of the window. Come on!*

Oli, at the next table to Brianna's, is fidgeting, looking around, trying to catch his classmates' eyes. Maisie, on the other side of the classroom, has lowered her head and shut her eyes.

❝ *Come on, Brianna! Wake up! Can't answer? Why doesn't that surprise me? Okay, who shall we have next? Let's see...*

Oli swings round in his chair and shoves his neighbour, then laughs.

❝ *Oli! What do you think you're doing? This isn't a zoo. Sit up! You can answer the question for us.*

❝ *No! Answer it yourself!*

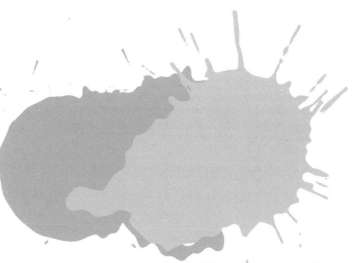

Strategy: If the learner assumes they can't do the task

This is about a lack of confidence that may have built up even in very young children, leading them to think of themselves as a failure. They may be saying to themselves: *'Why bother trying to do this? I know I'll make a mess of it. I'm no good at learning and stuff like that.'* And if they're not bothering to try, their energy may go into disruptive behaviour instead. Your task here is to challenge this mindset so that the learner regains their confidence and motivation. Don't save your praise only for achievement. You can build confidence by praising effort, too.

11. Yes we can!

Praise is a great reward, and sometimes as teachers we have to create opportunities to praise learners who might otherwise never begin to earn it. You don't always have to reserve your praise for success. You can praise learners for trying, or for having a go at answering a question, even if they get it wrong. You can praise them for acts of courtesy, such as holding the door, saying please or thank you or letting someone else go first. You can praise them for tidiness or cheerfulness. Praise builds confidence and can begin to dispel those self-perpetuating beliefs some learners have about being sure to fail.

12. Small steps

Another way to build learners' confidence and create opportunities to praise them is by breaking down the tasks you set them into small, bite-sized, easily achievable steps. You can then give them plenty of praise as they achieve each one. As the praise accumulates, it accustoms the learner to feeling a sense of achievement, which is a reward in itself.

Compare these two teachers' use of praise: praise for effort or praise only for success. Which is the more likely to give disengaged learners the confidence to join in positively with lessons?

Teacher A:

" *So which of these two go together? Angel, would you like to tell me?*

Angel:

" *Is it those two?*

Teacher A:

" *That's a good try. It's almost right. Well done, Angel. Finlay, do you want to have a go?*

Finlay:

" *Is it that one and then the one on the end?*

Teacher A:

" *That's so close. Two answers so far that are very close. But we're not quite there yet. Well tried, Finlay. Thank you. What about you, Lilly? Do you want a go?*

Lilly:

" *No.*

Teacher A:

" *Okay. That's okay. No worries, Lilly. How about Sunjeev? Do you want a go?*

Sunjeev:

" *Is it the one on the end and the third one?*

Teacher A:

" *That's right! The one on the end and this one, number three. Well done, Sunjeev. Thank you. And thank you everybody who had a go. And you, Lilly. It wasn't easy, was it?*

Teacher B:

" *So which of these two go together? Angel, you tell me.*

Angel:

" *Is it those two?*

Teacher B:

" *Nope. Finlay?*

Finlay:

" *Is it that one and then the one on the end?*

Teacher B:

" *No. You've obviously not been listening either. Lilly?*

Lilly:

" *I don't want to.*

Teacher B:

" *What do you mean, you don't want to? I'm asking you a question. No? You don't know either? Hasn't anybody been listening? Sunjeev? How about you?*

Sunjeev:

" *Is it the one on the end and the third one?*

Teacher B.

" *About time. Yes. It's those two. Good. At least somebody's been listening.*

Strategy: If the learner would rather be somewhere else

Sometimes it may seem to you as though a learner would rather be anywhere else but in the classroom, and this may be true. It could be that they have no interest in what they're supposed to be learning or – indeed – in learning anything at all. Or it could be that they're restless, unused to sitting still or being in one place for any length of time, simmering with unused energy and desperate to let off steam.

13. Where do we start?

Sometimes it's inevitable that a subject, a topic or an activity will hold no interest for a learner. One way to address this is to start with what *does* interest them and build the learning experience around that as far as possible. If they like Star Wars, get it in there somehow. It's not easy, in these days of prescriptive curriculum content, to use the learners' interests as your starting point. But, with a bit of imagination and ingenuity, it's not impossible. And it's well worth the effort.

14. Take a break

Build mini-breaks into your lesson. Ask learners to stand up and shake themselves, or run on the spot or touch their toes three times or stand up and then sit down three times quickly. These mini-breaks may be only 30 seconds long, so they won't take up valuable learning time. Rather, they can make the time spent on learning much more effective. As we've already discussed, learners have a limited span of concentration. Often, the younger they are, the shorter this may be. But even some learners in their teens may find it difficult to concentrate on one task or topic for more than five minutes or so. You may find it useful to build in mini-breaks (or a change of activity) as frequently as every 15 minutes – which is about the average attention span.

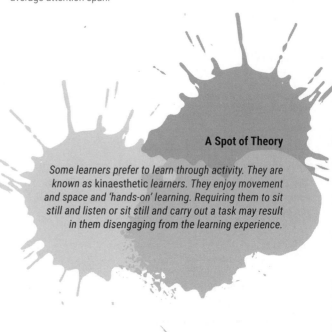

A Spot of Theory

Some learners prefer to learn through activity. They are known as kinaesthetic *learners. They enjoy movement and space and 'hands-on' learning. Requiring them to sit still and listen or sit still and carry out a task may result in them disengaging from the learning experience.*

Take a few moments to jot down ideas for a subject which is likely to capture your learners' interest as a starting point for your next lesson. Whether it's Star Wars, small furry animals, Pokémon, Big Brother, dinosaurs, rap, or whatever else, think about how it could be used as a context for teaching either your specialist subject or any two of the following:

* measuring;
* social justice;
* spelling;
* safety at work;
* number;
* European history;
* art and design;
* environmental issues;
* respect and responsibility;
* Shakespeare;
* phonics;
* PE.

Capture your learners' interest

Strategy: If the learner thinks *you'd* rather be somewhere else

We can't expect learners to feel enthusiastic about their lessons if they're getting the impression that their teacher isn't and that you would probably rather be anywhere else at that moment than there in the classroom with them. And, let's face it, there are moments with a difficult class when it's hard to dredge up much enthusiasm. But this creates a cycle of negativity: the learners are disengaged, possibly behaving badly; the teacher looks fed up, clearly doesn't want to be there, doesn't seem to like them; the learners pick up on this and their behaviour becomes even more negative – and so on. So here are two ways to break this cycle and encourage positive engagement.

15. When you're smiling

Smile and look happy to be there. On some days, this may take some Oscar-winning acting skills on your part, but it will certainly pay off. Keep your sense of humour and take every opportunity to demonstrate it (but never unkindly or at the expense of a learner). Keep your interactions positive wherever possible. You need to convince the learners that you like them and enjoy being there with them. (You'll find lots of ideas about how to do this in later chapters.) All this may sound difficult. But it should get easier and easier as the learners begin to respond to your positivity by demonstrating more positive behaviour themselves.

16. Cheerleading

Look enthusiastic! You can't expect learners to feel interested in something if their teacher is clearly not. *Never* say, *'I know this is boring but we've got to do it'*. Always keep any misgivings you may have about the curriculum to yourself! Again, this may call for a star performance; but enthusiasm is infectious. The more you demonstrate it, the more likely you are to engage the interest (and, who knows? – even the enthusiasm) of the class.

Read these two teachers' comments. Which one is most likely to:

(a) encourage learners to want to listen, and

(b) get them in the mood to engage positively with the lesson?

Teacher A (scowling):

" Alright. Alright. I know you don't want to be doing this. I don't either. But you're going to have to do it so shut up and listen. Why are we doing it? Because we've got to do it. And I don't like it any more than you do. What are you laughing at, Darryl?

Teacher B (smiling):

" Okay everyone. Listen up. We've got some really interesting stuff to cover today. I've been looking forward to this. I think you're really going to enjoy it. I know I am. Who's ready for this? Give me a Yes? Everybody ready? I can see Darryl smiling. That's great! Here we go.

A Spot of Theory

Research suggests that, for learners – and particularly those aged 14 to 18 – the 'cheerfulness' of a teacher has a positive impact on behaviour and motivation. 'Cheerfulness' may include a good sense of humour as well as positive, friendly interactions with learners. Details of this research can be found in Wallace, S (2014) When You're Smiling: Exploring How Teachers Motivate and Engage Learners in the Further Education Sector. Journal of Further and Higher Education, 38(3): 346–60.

If you only try one thing from this chapter, try this*

Use this to keep a record of what worked well for you and what didn't. A strategy that works with one class may not work so well with another. Keeping a checklist helps you to work out what factors or learner characteristics call for one approach rather than another. There's a line at the bottom for you to add your own most frequently used strategy, if it's not already included in the list.

Strategy	Tried it with...	On...(date)	It worked	It didn't work	Worth trying again?
1. Easy peasy?					
2. Expert-ease					
3. Diversify					
4. Getting to know you					
5. Step back					
6. Vive la difference					
7. Nothing personal					
8. Breaking the cycle					
9. Safety in numbers					
10. No pouncing					
11. Yes we can!					
12. Small steps					
13. Where do we start?					
14. Take a break					
15. When you're smiling*					
16. Cheerleading					
Your own strategy?					

DAY 3: Avoiding escalation: dealing with non-compliance and confrontation

Non-compliant or confrontational?

If a learner is not doing what you've asked them to do, or is doing something you've asked them *not* to do, they are being non-compliant. This can take many forms, from the primary school pupil who carries on wiping bogeys on a classmate, to the 17-year-old who spends his time gazing out of the window instead of getting on with the task in hand. One learner's non-compliance may disturb the learning process for others, while the non-disruptive kind – such as window gazing – may only impact negatively on the learning of the individual concerned. The teacher will often have to make a judgement, therefore, about how, and at what point, to intervene.

Confrontational behaviour, on the other hand, is always serious and can be very disruptive. It includes 'talking back'; using aggressive language or behaviour towards the teacher and/or classmates; or engaging in any behaviour purposely intended to draw the teacher into a dispute or difficult stand-off. Some forms of non-compliance can be directly confrontational – for example, the pupil who doesn't simply say, *'No!''* to a direct request, but adds (or implies), *'So what are you going to do about it?'*

There are three key points to remember here:

- ✸ While non-compliance can sometimes be described as 'low level', confrontation can't.
- ✸ When dealing with problem behaviour, it's very important to make sure that your intervention doesn't cause more disruption than the behaviour itself.
- ✸ It's important to deal with non-compliance in a way that will not make it escalate into open confrontation.

Today's strategies

- ✸ Tactical ignoring:
  1. Choose your battles
- ✸ Assumption of compliance:
  2. Who's the boss?
- ✸ Avoiding giving direct orders:
  3. Ways with words
- ✸ Avoiding threats:
  4. What not to say
- ✸ Negotiating rules:
  5. Entering negotiations
- ✸ Demonstrating the behaviour you'd like to see:
  6. Modelling

Strategy: Tactical ignoring

Sometimes, when dealing with non-compliance, you will be faced with a tricky decision. It goes like this: *If I intervene, will my intervention cause more disruption to learning than if I let the non-compliance continue and deal with it later, quietly, one-to-one with the culprit?* The reasoning behind this approach is simple and logical: If you have a class where most learners are working productively, with their attention fixed on the activity they've been given, it isn't a good idea to provide a small drama which will draw their attention away from their work and on to the fact that someone isn't actually on task. This is particularly important if you're pretty sure that, once you start, you'll have to keep intervening over and over again. Repeatedly and publically telling someone off, accentuating the negative, isn't a good idea when the majority of the class is working hard.

1. Choose your battles

It's far better to use your time and energy praising and encouraging the majority of the learners. Of course, you also have a duty towards the *non-compliant* learner or learners, to support, encourage and motivate them. But this may be best done afterwards or quietly, when it won't disturb the rest of the class, and can take the form of appropriate support rather than public nagging and criticism. It's important to remember that tactical ignoring can be justified only under certain circumstances; in other words when:

i) the non-compliant behaviour isn't interrupting anyone else's learning.

ii) you can reasonably be supposed not to have noticed it. (If it's obvious you've seen it but are ignoring it, this sends the wrong message to your class about what is and is not appropriate or acceptable behaviour.)

iii) you will engage with the non-compliant learner afterwards, both to support their learning and to make clear what behaviour is expected of them.

On the other hand, it is usually unwise to ignore *confrontational* behaviour. Ignoring visible, audible, public confrontations – whether these are directed at you or at other learners – is not a good idea. It sends out the wrong signals because it suggests that such behaviour is okay; that it will be tolerated; and that you, as the teacher, can't take control of what happens in the classroom. This can be a very disturbing idea for learners, particularly for young ones.

Consider the following five scenarios. Can you distinguish between the behaviour which is confrontational and that which is non-compliant? In which scenarios might tactical ignoring be a useful strategy? Remember to keep the following question in mind:

● **Would it be more disruptive for the majority of the class if I tactically ignore this behaviour or if I intervene?**

A. Let's start with an easy one. At the beginning of the chapter we saw two examples of non-compliance: the learner annoying her neighbour by wiping something nasty on his jumper, and the learner gazing out of the window instead of working. To make it more interesting, we'll change them round and say the wiper is 17 years old and the gazer is 6 years old. Which of these could be tactically ignored, and why?

B. Most of the class is working fairly quietly, but two learners are throwing screwed up pieces of paper at one another. Is this confrontational or non-compliant? Should you tactically ignore this?

C. You've noticed one learner is playing with her phone under the table, despite you having asked her to put it away. The rest are working quietly. Could you tactically ignore her?

D. The class is noisy but generally on task, apart from one table where the learners are talking about something they've seen on television and are not getting on with their task at all. Is this a case for tactical ignoring?

E. You ask one of your learners to move to another table because she has been talking to her neighbour, preventing her from working. She refuses to move, and keeps on talking. Can you tactically ignore it?

A Spot of Theory

Bill Rogers (b. 1947), an Australian educational consultant and behaviour specialist, emphasises that tactical ignoring should only be used in repeated *or* 'secondary' *instances of unacceptable behaviour. You can read more in his book,* Classroom Behaviour *(4th edition, Sage, 2015).*

Answers

☑ A. You can tactically ignore the gazer but not the wiper (because she's distracting someone else from learning).

☑ B. Non-compliant; but you can't ignore it: (a) because everyone's seen it, and (b) because they're disturbing the rest of the class.

☑ C. You can tactically ignore her if this would avoid a fuss likely to disturb the others.

☑ D. No. There are several of them. You have to get them back on task. The ambient noise means you won't disturb the others too much when you intervene.

☑ E. This is confrontation. You can't ignore it. And she's stopping a neighbour from learning.

Strategy: Assumption of compliance

Assumption of compliance sounds complicated, but is, in fact very simple; and it's a useful alternative strategy to tactical ignoring. It works like this:

2. Who's the boss?

If a learner is distracting others or breaking some rule of behaviour, you tell them what you want them to do or not do and then move quickly on to something else. You don't stand over them, waiting for them to comply. You don't give them more than the minimum of attention. You turn your attention, and that of the class, to something else immediately. This works in a number of ways.

* It demonstrates that you expect the learner to comply – that not to comply is not an acceptable option.

* It avoids rewarding the unwanted behaviour with too much attention.

* It demonstrates your confidence in your effectiveness as the person in charge.

* It keeps to a minimum the amount of attention the learner's behaviour gets from the rest of the class.

* The minimal intervention causes the minimum of disruption to learning.

* The class sees that you've noticed the behaviour and are dealing with it.

* Making only brief eye contact and moving on helps to avoid this escalating into a less manageable confrontation.

It is possible – even likely – that you will have to repeat the intervention several times. But it's important not to let the tone of your intervention escalate. You should say the same thing each time, calmly and firmly, preferably using the learner's name: *'I'd like you to put that away now and get on with your work, Caden.' 'I'd like you to go back to your seat and get on with your work, Lily.' 'I'd like you to stop shouting and talk quietly, Ollie.'* Don't linger or prolong your eye contact. Direct your attention immediately elsewhere – perhaps to praise other learners who are working hard, or perhaps to say something to the whole class. If you're walking about the classroom, you can apply this strategy as you're passing the learner in question. Like water dripping on a stone, this strategy will almost always make an impression in the end. But remember: while it's useful and effective in cases of non-compliance, it may not be appropriate in cases where behaviour is actively confrontational.

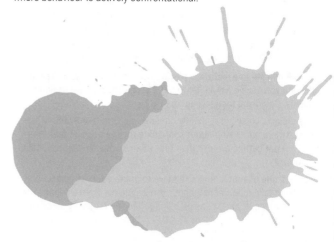

Here are two examples of teachers using the Assumption of Compliance strategy. One teacher is working with older learners, the other with primary pupils. As you read through the examples, consider whether the age of the learners is relevant when it comes to how this strategy is being implemented.

A. A class of 17 year olds at a further education college are working in groups on a project which is to be assessed. One learner, Ryan, is contributing nothing to his group. Instead, he is playing a game on his phone. The teacher is walking from group to group, asking and answering questions. When the teacher comes to Ryan's group, she says: *'Ryan, I'd like you to put that phone away, please.'* Then, immediately turning to the rest of the group, she says, *'This is coming along nicely. What did you decide to do about the questionnaire?'* The next time she passes this group she sees Ryan is still playing with his phone. She says, calmly, *'Ryan, I'd like you to put the phone away. I need to see you doing some work,'* and moves on to the next group. She repeats this once more as she comes round to Ryan's group again. This time, as she moves away, she hears another member of the group say, *'Yeah, come on, Ryan. Why should we be doing all this work for you?'* Ryan puts his phone away and joins in.

B. A class of Year 2 pupils have been asked to write a half-page story about the paper dragons they've been making. Lela has written only one line and keeps getting up and wandering over to look at the paper dragons that are laid out to dry. Some of the other pupils are anxious she will touch or 'spoil' their dragons. The teacher says, *'Leave those alone now, Lela. I'd like you to sit down and get on. Alisha, what lovely neat writing! Well done!'* Lela sits down but is soon getting to her feet again. The teacher walks past her table and – without stopping – says, *'I'd like you to sit down, please, Lela and do your writing.'* Later, Lela gets up again. The teacher says, calmly, *'Sit down, Lela, and get on with your writing. Five more minutes, everybody. Let's get finished in time for playtime. That's lovely work, Rory.'* Lela, perhaps catching on to the fact that there's not much of a pay-off from wandering about and realising that she might get more attention by staying put and finishing her writing, finally manages three or four lines by playtime.

It's important to bear in mind, of course, that if Ryan's or Lela's non-compliance was the result of difficulties they were experiencing with the level or the content of the task, an intervention would be necessary in the first instance to actively support their learning rather than to address their behaviour.

Strategy: Avoiding giving direct orders

One way to ensure that non-compliance doesn't escalate into open confrontation is to choose your words carefully when challenging a learner's behaviour. If you give a direct order, such as *'Sit down, now!'* or *'Go and stand over there!'* or *'Give me that, now!'*, you leave yourself open to being publically disobeyed – in which case, what started as non-compliance has suddenly escalated into confrontation. This doesn't help your morale, and it doesn't do much for class morale, either. One of the challenges we face as teachers is that we cannot, as individuals, 'enforce' orders. So it's best to avoid giving them. There are much more effective ways of communicating instructions to learners. For example:

3. Ways with words

● You can present an instruction as something you would like the learner to do. *'I'd like you to sit down now, Glen.' 'Alia, I'd like you to go and stand over there.' 'I'd like you to give me that now, Stefka.'* If the learner ignores this, you're still only dealing with non-compliance; the rest of the class hasn't had to witness direct defiance, and the situation hasn't escalated into a confrontational stand-off. You can then repeat the instruction in this form as often as necessary, using the Assumption of Compliance strategy.

● A variation on this is to add the words, *'for me'*. You've probably been on the receiving end of this yourself, at the doctor's or the hair salon, for example, *'Just look this way for me'*. It softens an order into a non-confrontational request, while making the instruction quite clear. You can hear the effect if you read the following out loud: *'Sit down for me now, Glen.' 'Stand over there for me, Alia.' 'Put that away for me now, Stefka.'*

● An alternative approach is to describe to the learner what it is that they're doing: *'You're wandering around again, Glen.' 'Alia, you're standing in the wrong place.' 'You're playing with your nails again, Stefka.'* Like the other examples, this is a non-confrontational approach, and is more likely to resolve the problem than to escalate it.

You are disappearing out of the window again class!

Have a look at these examples of teacher–learner interaction. Which ones do you think are likely to be most effective at getting Finlay to behave without escalation or confrontation?

Finlay is swinging about on his chair and talking to his neighbour Mo while the teacher is explaining something to the class. The teacher says:

Example A:

❝ *You're swinging on your chair, Finlay. I don't want you to fall and hurt yourself. I'd like you sit sensibly.*

Example B:

❝ *Sit still for me, please, Finlay, and leave Mo alone.*

Example C:

❝ *Finlay! Sit still and shut up!*

Example D:

❝ *I'd like you and Mo to hear what I'm saying, Finlay, because it's important. So sit sensibly on your chair for me and stop chattering.*

Example E:

❝ *Stop swinging about on your chair, Finlay. You'll tip it over. And leave Mo alone. He's trying to listen, even if you aren't.*

Here are some of the things you may have noticed about those examples:

Example A:

❝ The teacher chooses to address only one of the behaviours – the swinging about on the chair. Dealing with one behaviour at a time can be a useful way to apply this strategy. It keeps the instruction clear and focused, which can be important for young learners or those who are easily distracted. Here the teacher very sensibly chooses the safety issue as the one to focus on.

Example B:

❝ *'For me'* and *'please'* transform a confrontational order into a request, and also provide a model of courteous communication for the learner.

Example C:

❝ Oh dear! I'm not saying this will never work, but it's not a good idea. It's a declaration of war. It creates the danger of escalation (If Finlay doesn't comply, what happens next?) and it provides a very poor model of behaviour for the learner.

Example D:

❝ The instruction is given clearly and the reason for it is also clearly explained, which increases the chance of it working.

Example E:

❝ This is one to be avoided at all costs. It plants the idea of the chair falling over, which might immediately appeal to Finlay as his next move. And it seems to be telling him that the teacher has given up on him (*'He's trying to listen, even if you aren't.'*) Giving Finlay that sort of label is likely to make his behaviour worse, not better.

Strategy: Avoiding threats

Empty threats are a sign of weakness. They're dangerous, too, because they can be taken as a challenge.

Threats are a direct confrontation, and confrontation is something you don't want in your classroom. They also set a very bad example to your learners. It's like saying to them, *'Making threats is okay.'*

4. What not to say

When dealing with problem behaviour in the classroom:

* never make threats which you can't carry out (*'Stop that or I'll have you thrown out!'*);

* never imply threats which you can't carry out (*'Stop that now or you'll be sorry!'*);

* never play the prophet of doom and threaten future life-changing consequences (*'Keep behaving like that and you'll never get a job!'*).

A positive and much more effective approach is to encourage the learner to think out for themselves the consequences of their behaviour. This means asking questions such as:

* What do you think might happen if you keep doing that?

* How do you think your Mum/Dad/ carer might feel if we have to write them a letter about your behaviour?

* What are we going to be able to write in a reference for you if you don't show us you can behave responsibly?

* What do you think would happen if you were at work and kept doing that?

The key here is that the questions should be asked conversationally, not angrily. If you ask them angrily, your anger is all that you'll communicate. Your immediate aim is to encourage the learner to think and reflect. Your longer-term goal is that they learn to consider the consequences before they act and so begin to take control of their own behaviour.

Let's imagine that a learner is running around, or playing around, with something sharp. If it's a younger pupil it might be a sharpened pencil, or – in the case of an older learner – it might be scissors or a workshop tool. The teacher's first impulse might be to say something like:

" *Stop running around with that! You'll hurt someone! You'll hurt yourself! I'll take it off you if you keep doing that!*

The learner may, or may not stop.

What have they learnt?

- That the teacher will tell them when something is dangerous.
- Spotting danger is the teacher's responsibility.
- They – the learner – aren't responsible for seeing when something is dangerous.

Compare this with the following approach. The teacher resists that first knee-jerk reaction to shout a warning and a threat. Instead, they say something like:

" *Loyola, I'd like you to come here, please. Walking, not running. Thank you. Can you see how sharp that is? What do you think could happen if you run or play about with it?*

The learner has stopped. The teacher can take it from there.

What has Loyola learnt?

- That the teacher expects her to think about her own behaviour and its consequences.
- That the teacher treats her as capable of thinking things out for herself.
- That the teacher wants her to recognise what's dangerous because the teacher is concerned for learners' safety.

Strategy: Negotiating rules

The rules for behaviour which a school or college sets out in their behaviour policy are non-negotiable, of course. And the law of the land will always apply. But in your classroom you do have leeway to set some additional basic ground rules, and you'll find these are easier to apply if you've involved the learners in drawing them up. The agreed rules should be displayed prominently. You'll find that the learners' sense of ownership over these rules means that they'll do some of the 'policing' themselves.

5. Entering negotiations

It's useful to negotiate rules in two categories: things the learners should do (such as settling down when you ask for quiet) and things they shouldn't do (such as running around in the classroom or – depending on the age group – swearing). As the teacher, you have the veto over any silly suggestions for rules – and they *will* certainly try it on with some silly ones to start with. And, in the spirit of negotiation, you can also suggest rules yourself if the learners haven't come up with some of the basic ones you want in there.

As an extension to this strategy, you might like to appoint two or more learners each week to take a lead in policing the rules. A good idea is to choose those who have kept to the rules the best in the previous week. Alternatively, you can let the class vote for who's going to police them. But present that option with caution, and be prepared to veto unsuitable candidates.

Negotiated rules can cover things such as:

- who talks when;
- communicating in the classroom – courtesy and politeness;
- health and safety;
- no shouting;
- no fighting;
- no 'talking back';
- noise levels;
- choices about who works with whom;
- punctuality;
- behaviour while entering and leaving the classroom.

The list will depend very much on the age and characteristics of those particular learners. But negotiated rules are worth trying as an effective strategy whether your learners are 5 or 50 years old.

A Spot of Theory

Negotiating rules with learners gives them ownership and makes them feel their input is valued. It treats them as valued partners in the learning process, rather than making them feel that learning is something that's done to them. Humanist psychologists such as Carl Rogers (1902–1987) emphasise the importance of showing learners that they are valued, and stress the impact this can have on their motivation to learn.

Strategy: Demonstrating the behaviour you'd like to see

If you want your learners to behave appropriately, cheerfully and courteously, you will need to provide them with the most effective and permanently available role model – you, yourself.

6. Modelling

If you want your class to be enthusiastic about the subject or topic they're working on, then you have to demonstrate your own enthusiasm – whether you're actually feeling it that day or not. And if you want your learners to be less rowdy, you won't help the situation by shouting at them. Similarly, if you lose your temper with them, it makes it harder to ask them to control their own feelings of anger and aggression. There's nothing wrong with showing that you are angry if that anger is justified. But that's a very different thing to losing your temper. Losing your temper demonstrates a loss of control. You can't expect the learners to control their behaviour if you can't always control yours. And while it's fine to show that there are some behaviours you don't like and will discourage, it's never okay to show that you don't like your learners. Smile and look pleased to see them. That way you just might get them to smile back.

Some ways of modelling positive behaviour

- Always look pleased to be there.
- Be enthusiastic about the subject or topic.
- Treat all learners with respect.
- Demonstrate appropriate use of language.
- Don't shout unless absolutely necessary.
- Listen to them when they tell you something (because that's what you want them to do when *you're* talking).
- Demonstrate your sense of humour – be prepared to lighten up and laugh.
- Take your learners' concerns seriously.

In the following scenario there are at least ten ways in which the teacher is setting a poor example and sending the wrong messages about what is acceptable behaviour. They are all behaviours or attitudes she would certainly criticise her learners for.

● **Can you spot them?**

● **What impression is she giving to the class in terms of how she feels about them?**

● **What would you do differently?**

The teacher is busy sorting resources out and so the class gets noisy. She has her back to them. She turns her head and shouts,

" *Be quiet and sit down!*

After a while she turns her attention to the class and shouts again,

" *I told you to sit down! Quiet! You two over there! I said quiet!*

The noise subsides a little bit and she says,

" *Listen carefully! What we're going to do now is difficult and it's complicated. If you don't listen you won't be able to do it. Yes, Jan, I know it's boring. But we have to do it. I don't like it any more than you do. Here. Give these out.*

She tosses a pile of worksheets to a learner on the front table.

" *Come on! Are you deaf? Hurry up! We don't want to be doing this all day. I've got better things to do! Jan! What are you smiling at? There's nothing to smile about!*

Answers

☑ She doesn't start on time (unpunctual)

☑ She keeps her back to them (rude)

☑ She shouts orders at them (noisy)

☑ She uses 'you two' instead of names (discourteous)

☑ She makes the topic sound too difficult for them (insults them)

☑ She tell them it's boring (oh dear!)

☑ She throws the worksheets (throwing things)

☑ She uses a disability as an insult (unacceptable language and behaviour)

☑ She tells them she doesn't want to be there (so why should they?)

☑ She discourages smiling (implying that learning is a negative experience)

Checklist

Use this to keep a record of what worked well for you and what didn't. A strategy that works with one class may not work so well with another. Keeping a checklist helps you to work out what factors or learner characteristics call for one approach rather than another. There's a line at the bottom for you to add your own most frequently used strategy, if it's not already included in the list.

Strategy	Tried it with...	On...(date)	It worked	It didn't work	Worth trying again?
1. Choose your battles					
2. Who's the boss?					
3. Ways with words					
4. What not to say					
5. Entering negotiations★					
6. Modelling					
Your own strategy?					

DAY 4: Won't listen; can't listen: dealing with noise

Good noise or bad noise?

First of all, let's be clear about what we mean by *noise*. As teachers, we all know from experience that a noisy classroom is not necessarily an unproductive classroom. Sometimes noise is a necessary component of the learning process, whether it's the learner talk essential to activities like groupwork and discussion, or the use of essential learning resources, from music to machinery. And we also know that the more learners become engaged with a group task, for example, the more animated their talking is likely to get. This means that the volume of learner talk can actually be a barometer of how much learning is taking place – in a good way.

There's the question, too, of tolerance levels. What *you* might describe as a productive buzz of learner activity, Ofsted might label *'low-level disruption'*, and your colleague in the next classroom might call an unacceptable level of noise. So what we need is a rule of thumb to help us recognise when to intervene in order to bring noise levels down. And it's this:

Noise is a problem when it becomes a barrier to learning.

In practical terms, this means it's a problem when learners:

* can't hear (or aren't listening to) what you're saying;

* are talking 'off task', not engaging with the lesson;

* are making it impossible for other learners to work effectively;

* are disturbing other classrooms;

* are generating noise which feels aggressive or threatening to you or others.

The noise may be low level rather than dramatic; but if it's causing these sorts of problems, you will need to address it. Today's strategies are designed to help you do that.

Today's strategies

* Getting off to an orderly start:
  1. Meet and greet
  2. Straight down to business: no time to chat

* Grabbing and keeping their attention:
  3. Sparkle
  4. Pace
  5. All change

* Using (and not using) your voice:
  6. Softly softly
  7. The silent wait

* Organising the environment:
  8. Eyes front
  9. Mixing it up
  10. Back row seats

* Using rewards and sanctions to keep noise down:
  11. Rewards and how to use them
  12. Setting up sanctions

* Working together:
  13. Peer pressure

Strategy: Getting off to an orderly start

It's much easier to overcome the problem of a noisy classroom if you can prevent noise building up in the first place. Getting the lesson off to an orderly start is the key to success. To ensure this happens, a couple of factors are essential.

* *You need to be there already when the learners arrive.* (If you're teaching in primary education this, of course, is a given. But in secondary and further education, where learners and teachers are moving around the institution independently from one classroom to another, it's not always easy to achieve.)

* *You need to start your lesson promptly with a noise-busting activity.*

Then you're ready to implement the dual Orderly Start strategy, which goes like this:

1. Meet and greet

Stand by the door and greet your learners as they come in. Greet as many as you can by name. Look pleased to see them all. Personalise your welcome in a positive way wherever you can. For example:

" *Good morning, Ryan. That was a nice piece of work you did for me yesterday/last week.*

" *Hello, Mo. You're looking very cheerful today.*

" *Come in, Bella. Well done for working so hard yesterday.*

Obviously, it's impossible to speak to every individual, especially when the learners come barreling in, as they often do. But the ones you don't address directly will still hear what's being said to the others. So the Meet and Greet strategy works in a number of ways:

* It establishes your effective presence right from the start.

* It reminds them that you're in charge.

* It says: *'Switch off the chatter now. The lesson starts here!'*

* It breaks up conversations that may have started in the corridor.

* It gets the lesson off to a positive start.

2. Straight down to business: no time to chat

An engaging activity right at the start of the lesson cuts down the opportunity for chatter and noise to build. There are three essentials here: it needs to be implemented immediately, require them to concentrate, and be relevant to their learning. Here are some ideas:

" *I'm going to play you a four-minute clip from YouTube about [whatever they did the previous lesson/day/week] and I want you to watch and listen carefully and note down the different words they use to describe [X].*

" *Two teams. This side of the room versus that side of the room. We're going to have a six-minute quiz about what we did last lesson/ yesterday/last week. Any shouting out and the point goes to the other side.*

" *On your tables you'll each find a diagram of [something covered last lesson/yesterday/last week]. I want you to label it correctly and add and label anything you think is missing. You've got ten minutes, starting **now**.*

A noisy start to a lesson can look (and sound) something like this:

Teacher (loudly):
" *Okay everybody. Settle down!*

Noise continues.
Teacher (louder):
" *That'll do. Settle down now. Bella, that's enough.*

Noise continues.
Teacher (shouting):
" *Come on, everybody! That's enough! Settle down. Mo! I said settle down. Now!*

Noise continues.
Teacher (shouting more loudly and clapping hands):
" *I SAID QUIET! RYAN! STOP TALKING AND TURN TO THE FRONT!*

Now, compare this start to what's happening in the Meet and Greet strategy on the previous page. There, instead of kicking off noisily with the teacher and learners on opposing sides, the lesson starts in a friendly, positive mood. Instead of having to begin with criticism and 'telling off', the teacher is able to establish a positive mood, handing out approval and praise. Instead of having to raise their voice, modelling exactly the behaviour they *don't* want from the learners, the teacher is able to communicate pleasantly in a normal speaking voice – because that's the best example to set the learners.

For the No Time to Chat follow-up, sometimes called a 'settling activity', there are plenty of possibilities. As well as those on the previous page, you could set learners the task of spotting mistakes in pictures or text; or matching pictures/diagrams to relevant words.

NB: If you have a class who are particularly difficult to settle down, you might consider offering a prize for successful completion.

A Spot of Theory

The psychologist, Abraham Maslow (1908–1970), tells us that learning won't effectively take place unless the learner feels comfortable and safe. A positive welcome and an orderly start to the lesson will provide the reassurance that they are in safe hands.

Strategy: Grabbing and keeping their attention

3. Sparkle

If learners are chatting among themselves rather than listening to you, it may be that they find that more interesting than what you have to say or how you are saying it. Adding some extra sparkle to your teaching style can make a big difference. Here are some ways to do it:

- **Look and sound enthusiastic. Some days this will call for you to use your acting skills, but it'll be worth it.**

- **Don't talk AT them. A monologue from the teacher can cause learners to switch off and talk among themselves. So make it a conversation as far as you possibly can, by asking and inviting questions, drawing them in, giving them an opportunity to talk – but to you and the rest of the class rather than just to their neighbours.**

- **Look happy to be there and *smile*. This sounds so simple and you've heard it before; and yet you'll be amazed at how well it can work to draw learners' attention to you rather than each other.**

- **Make as much eye contact with as many of them as possible. This draws them in and keeps their attention on you.**

- **Surprise them. Don't be predictable. If they know you always stand by your desk, or walk up and down by the whiteboard or pay more attention to the left side of the room, you might as well be wallpaper – and they'll soon begin to ignore you.**

4. Pace

When you've got the class straight down to business with an activity that gives them no time to start growing noisy (see previous page: No Time to Chat), you should make sure you follow up by keeping the pace going. Pace is very important if you want to avoid learners growing bored and making their own noisy amusement (The Victorians had a doom-laden saying they were fond of, which was: *The Devil finds work for idle hands!*) Some useful ways of keeping up the pace are to:

- **Impose clear and fairly tight time constraints on all tasks. Give a clearly audible warning countdown as the end of the allowed time approaches. *'You have five more minutes to complete the task... You now have four more minutes...'* and so on. This keeps learners focused on the task because it introduces an element of non-threatening competition – them against the clock.**

- **Have relevant follow-on tasks prepared to give to learners who finish individual or group tasks early. This way, no one is sitting (or wandering about) with nothing to do.**

5. All change

To reliably hold learners' attention you will need to incorporate frequent changes of activity into your lesson plan. Remember that an average attention span – the time we are comfortable focusing on one topic or activity – is around 15–20 minutes. For younger learners this can be much less. After this time, the attention will wander. Regular changes of learning activity, therefore, can be very effective in keeping learners focused, engaged and settled.

A. Take particular notice of your own behaviour next time you teach a lesson, and try to evaluate your performance as honestly and objectively as possible against the following checklist. (Award yourself a mark out of ten for each category.)

- How animated is your body language?
- How enthusiastic do you appear about the topic?
- How happy do you look to be there?
- Are you making eye contact with the learners?
- Are you engaging them in conversation with questions and answers, allowing them their say, rather than doing all the talking yourself?
- How would you score yourself overall for 'sparkle'?

This is a useful way of finding out what you could be working on to put even more sparkle into your teaching. Perhaps you'll score ten out of ten across the board, in which case your learners are very lucky!

B. Imagine you are watching a colleague teach. She has divided the class into five groups and set them a group task. She has given them 15 minutes to complete it. After 10 minutes she begins the audible countdown, but two groups have already finished and have begun talking among themselves. The noise is growing louder and it looks as though it's distracting the three groups who are still not finished. She hands out an extension task to the ones who've finished, but – in your view – she's missed the moment. The noise is well established now and it's hard to get the learners back on task. At the end of the lesson she asks your advice. What would you suggest that she does differently next time?

A Spot of Theory

'As well as keeping up interest and pace, frequent changes of activity can also help to optimize learning. As any experienced teacher will tell you, learners will usually benefit from being exposed to a range of learning experiences: not only ones which require them to sit still and listen, but also activities which involve seeing and doing.'

(Wallace, S. (2013) Teaching in Further Education: The Inside Story. *Northwich: Critical Publishing.)*

Strategy: Using (and not using) your voice

6. Softly softly

When you're talking to a noisy class there's a natural tendency to raise your voice in order to be heard. Sometimes this works. But with a determinedly rowdy group it can be counter-productive. Sometimes – strange as this might sound – the most effective strategy is to speak more softly. Here are the reasons why:

- Raising your voice can just create escalation. You try to shout over them, so they raise the volume. So you have to shout louder, and they raise the volume again. And so on...

- Being loud is exactly what you want to discourage. If you get loud, you're setting a negative example. (Just picture a teacher yelling, *'I DON'T WANT TO HEAR ANY SHOUTING!'*)

- Feeling forced to shout over your learners is allowing them to set the volume in the classroom. Remember, you're the one in charge here.

- The more they get used to you shouting, the easier it'll be for them to ignore it.

- If you speak more softly, two things are likely to happen: (1) learners will have to quieten down so they can hear you; and (2) when they see you are saying something but can't quite hear what it is, some learners will begin 'shushing' the rest. This creates peer pressure, one of the most effective forms of behaviour management.

7. The silent wait

This takes some nerve and can be difficult for new or trainee teachers, but sometimes the most effective thing to do with your voice is to stop using it for a minute or two. Standing silently in front of a noisy class may seem difficult at first, but the pay-off can be well worth it. When learners see you waiting patiently, looking perfectly relaxed and with a smile on your face, they know you are ready to begin. In most cases, the one or two who notice first will begin to shush the others (peer pressure again). When the class is quiet enough to hear you without you having to raise your voice unduly, you can say, *'Thank you'*, and begin.

- Your silence sends a signal to the learners. It says: *I'm ready to begin and I have confidence in you that you'll notice this and settle down.*

- The smile is very important. Your smile says: *I'm happy to be here. I like you. I'm not intimidated by your noise.* The *'Thank you'* is a model for them of polite behaviour.

- Waiting patiently for a minute or two and looking relaxed about it says: *I'm comfortable being here with you in this classroom because I'm the one in charge.*

Speaking softly is a strategy you can use at any point in the lesson. The Silent Wait strategy is most often employed at the beginning of a lesson, but can also be useful when you need to regain learners' attention at the end of some group activity.

Like all strategies, these have their limitations, and very occasionally it will be necessary – even advisable – to raise your voice. Look at the following scenarios. Are there any here in which Softly Softly or the Silent Wait would be inappropriate?

- It has taken you a little while to set up the data projector – or perhaps you have some other problem with technology – and meanwhile the class has grown
  quite noisy. Now you're ready to begin, how do you get the noise down so that the lesson can proceed?

- Your learners have been doing project work in groups. You gave them 20 minutes for the task and the time is now up. The noise level has risen to a point where you're worrying that teachers in neighbouring classrooms might complain. What's the best way to get the class listening again?

- You are taking a class for another teacher. The learners' behaviour is quite unruly. Some of them at the back of the room are laughing and talking loudly, tipping their chairs back, trying to put their feet on the table. You're aware of how dangerous this is. This needs immediate action. What do you do?

- You need to give the class some essential information. Most of them are talking among themselves. What strategy could you use to get them to listen?

A Spot of Theory

Psychologists (eg, Geoff Beattie, 2004) have pointed out how we tend naturally, under certain circumstances, to mirror the body language of others. You can test this for yourself. If you are talking to someone and nodding (or folding your arms or leaning forward) they will probably, quite unconsciously, find themselves doing the same. This is why we should always try to model the behaviour we'd like our learners to adopt. And that includes looking relaxed, polite and not shouting!

Answer

 If learners are endangering themselves or others, a shouted warning may be necessary. But remember: shouting is an aggressive form of communication. In the long run, effective classroom behaviour management depends on building positive relationships.

Strategy: Organising the environment

8. Eyes front

Learners won't know that you need them to listen unless they can see you. You won't be able to hold their attention unless you can make eye contact with them all at the same time. The seating arrangement can sometimes make this difficult, particularly in infant/primary and in further education where learners tend to be grouped at tables. In those cases, you need to make sure that no learners are sitting with their backs to you. If getting them to move once they're seated looks as though it's going to be a problem, get in there first and shift chairs so there are none facing away from you. Or you can make sure the first activity on your lesson plan gets them looking voluntarily in your direction – eg watching something interesting on a screen – so they move their own seats around to see. Or you can use an activity that allows you to give reluctant movers a role they'll like which requires them to get up and roam or sit elsewhere. Being able to make eye contact with all learners at the same time is an essential first step in gaining the class's attention.

9. Mixing it up

Sometimes, if the noise is coming from particular pairs or groups of learners, the best solution is to split them up. This can be problematic when you're dealing with older learners who may be resistant to the idea of sitting somewhere else and not being with their mates. To avoid cries of *'It's not fair! You're picking on me and not her!'*, a useful strategy is to employ groupwork which involves dividing the class up in a way which appears random; for example, giving each learner a number by counting heads one, two, three, four, five and repeating until all are counted. Then you instruct all the 'ones' to form a group, all the 'twos' to do the same, and so on. This will split up individuals who, when together, tend to create pockets of noise.

10. Back row seats

Sometimes you may want to move particularly noisy and disruptive learners to somewhere they'll create less nuisance. Or you may, with younger learners, want to establish the equivalent of a 'naughty step'. There's a natural tendency to get these learners sitting where you can observe them most closely, at the front of the class. However, this is a risky strategy and can backfire. From the front they can vie with you for the class's attention. They're in a prime position to continue their performance. They now have an audience for any noise they want to make, and any continuing efforts you make to quieten them down become entertainment for the whole class. So, counter-intuitive as it sounds, often the best place to put them is at the back of the class. *You* can still keep an eye on them, but they're now out of their classmates' line of sight.

Have a look at the following three scenarios and decide which of the three strategies might be effective for reducing the noise.

A. You are briefing the class for a group task but some learners are finding it difficult to hear you because of the persistent talking going on among one group of girls. What do you do?

B. The classroom is set up with 12 trapezoid-shaped tables arranged as a group of six hexagons, three down each side of the classroom. When your 36 learners are all seated it is unavoidable that six of them will have their backs to you so that you find yourself addressing the backs of their heads. Unable to make or maintain eye contact with them, you find it difficult to prevent them talking when they need to be listening. How do you solve this problem?

C. One learner persists in interrupting and distracting his neighbours, despite three warnings from you. What could you do in this situation?

A Spot of Theory

Psychologists tell us that eye contact is an important factor in establishing rapport and trust. They also tell us that there is a direct correlation between teacher–learner eye contact and learner engagement. So eye contact may be the single most important factor in establishing classroom control. Allowing learners to sit facing away from you, your desk or whiteboard, even if you regularly move about the room, is simply asking for trouble (TESL Journal, Vol. X, No. 8, August 2004).

Answer

☑ A. Go smoothly into the Mixing It Up numbering off for groups strategy, thus splitting up the talkers without drawing attention to them. Then finish the briefing when the class is reseated in their allocated groups and can hear you without interruption. B. If asking learners to squeeze up meets with resistance, give them something they'll voluntarily move to see, like a topic-relevant YouTube clip. If necessary, shift tables apart into 12 smaller ones. Anything to get eyes front! C. Move the disruptive learner to the back of the class where it's difficult for him to distract anybody. Or, if you worry that asking him to move could trigger an even bigger distraction in the form of a confrontation, just implement the Mixing It Up strategy.

Strategy: Using rewards and sanctions to keep noise down

This strategy works by rewarding learners for the behaviour you want to see – in this case, not making an unnecessary amount of noise – and applying sanctions when they behave in an inappropriate way – for example, being unnecessarily noisy, rowdy or disruptive. Encouraging good behaviour with rewards is relatively straightforward. Finding effective sanctions to apply, however, means you will have to do some preparatory setting up. You may have heard this strategy referred to as *the carrot and the stick* approach. However, learners these days won't do much for a carrot; and a stick is, of course, completely out of the question.

11. Rewards and how to use them

To reward individuals, groups or whole classes for keeping the sound down you can use:

* smiles;
* eye contact;
* praise;
* music while they work;
* a fun activity for the final ten minutes of the lesson;
* special responsibility;
* sweets;
* star of the week;
* 'good conduct' certificates or badges;
* allowing a short, off-task break (5 mins max) for chat.

12. Setting up sanctions

To find effective and practical sanctions you will need to be inventive. Sending culprits to someone scarier than you and higher up the chain of command isn't something you want to be doing too often. Detentions, isolations or a lost break/playtime require additional supervision and may not take place immediately after the offence. The most effective sanction is a withheld or withdrawn reward. So, for example, if they make too much noise you won't allow music while they work; or they'll forfeit the fun activity they could have had at the end of the lesson; or their good conduct badge or special responsibility will be taken from them; or they'll fail to win the five minutes of chat time. In practical terms, these sanctions are straightforward to apply, once you have set up your system of rewards. In fact, the promise of a reward works as both an *incentive ('keep the noise down and you'll be rewarded')* and as a *warning ('make too much noise and look what you'll be missing out on')*. In other words, the sanction you'll be using is 'no reward'. This puts the outcome in the learners' own hands. And it's very important that you make sure they understand this.

Imagine that you are observing the following lesson. Look at the teacher's use of rewards and sanctions.

● **Does he always use them effectively?**

● **Are there any missed opportunities where he could have applied this strategy but doesn't?**

The class starts off in quite a chaotic way. It takes some time for the teacher to get the learners to settle down. Eventually he does so by promising them a short 'chat break' later if they now get down to work quietly. Most of the class quieten down, listen and then set to work on the task they've been given. One table is still making a noise which has nothing to do with the learning task. They are discussing loudly the merits of various online games. The teacher warns them that they won't get the 'chat break' if they don't get down to work. He walks around the room, chatting and smiling with the groups who are working well, and praising their efforts. Now and again he turns to the noisy group, who are still being loud, and frowns. Eventually the noisy group say that they'd be able to concentrate better on the task if he'll allow them some music. He agrees. The music plays. The group quietens down. At the end of the task the teacher allows all the class the promised five-minute 'chat break'.

A Spot of Theory

The theory which underpins reward and sanction has its origins in the work of B F Skinner (1904–1990) and the group of experimental psychologists we now refer to as neo-behaviourists. It draws on the idea of positive reinforcement – *rewarding a desired behaviour in order to encourage its repetition. This process is known as* behaviour modification. *Similarly, negative reinforcement – the withholding of reward – is used to discourage undesirable behaviour.*

Answers

☑ The promise of a 'chat break' reward works for most of the class.

☑ The threatened sanction of a no 'chat break' doesn't work for the noisy group. We soon see why! It's because he doesn't stick to it. They get their chat break after all, despite being noisy for much of the lesson. This was the wrong sanction to threaten them with, because in practical terms how could he allow most of the class five minutes to chat and yet keep that one small group from chatting? (A more effective sanction would be to say that NO ONE gets a chat break unless EVERYONE keeps the noise down. This would put peer pressure on the noisy group.)

☑ He uses the rewards of praise, smiling and eye contact with the rest of the class, keeping them motivated to stay on task. But his disapproving frowns don't work with the noisy group.

☑ The noisy group turns the tables on him by offering *him* the reward of them working quietly if he'll allow music! He's lost the initiative here. He could have offered them the reward of music earlier in the lesson. Now he's set the precedent of them being able to bribe him into allowing music on demand. They've modified his behaviour instead of him modifying theirs!

Strategy: Working together

If you've ever sat in a well-lit theatre before a show, and then listened to what happens when the lights go down and the curtain begins to rise, you'll have heard the audience chatter dying away and a few voices saying 'Ssshhh!' from here and there in the auditorium to silence the few who are still finishing their conversation or rattling their popcorn. And it usually works very well. There's rarely any need for a Stage Manager to walk out into the spotlight and urge the audience to be quiet so that the show can begin, because peer pressure alone has been sufficient. If some members of the audience make a noise, other members of the audience will 'shush' them. And that's exactly what you're aiming for in this strategy: to get the majority of the class working with you to keep the noisy ones reasonably quiet. You'll achieve this by setting up peer pressure.

13. Peer pressure

The use of peer pressure links very closely to the use of rewards and sanctions. Having read the answers on the previous page, you'll know by now that the teacher in the Rewards and Sanctions scenario missed the opportunity to exert peer pressure when offering the reward of the chat break. If he had said something like:

> **"** *As long as you ALL work quietly with no shouting and no messing about, you'll all get a five-minute chat break at the end of the task. But if there's any shouting or loud behaviour from ANYBODY, then there'll be no chat break for ANYONE, I'm afraid.*

The important words here are *all*, *anybody* and *anyone*. There may initially be cries of *'Unfair!'* but that doesn't matter. What you have done is to shift the dynamics in the room. The possibility of a reward is now in the learners' hands, not yours. The learners who want the reward and are willing to work for it will have a natural interest in keeping the rest – the noisy ones – from spoiling their chances. You can now hand the nagging and shushing (if these become necessary) over to them. And you'll probably already have noticed how learners who may be resistant to doing what the teacher tells them to do will buckle very quickly in order to keep on the right side of their peers. It's very rare for young learners to want to be unpopular with their classmates. This is something you can use and put to good effect.

A word of warning

It's absolutely essential to keep a balance here and not to let peer pressure tip over into bullying. The peer pressure strategy can be a positive and useful one, but must not be allowed to build into a situation where teacher and class could be perceived as 'ganging up' on one or two individual learners – particularly if those learners are already isolated or unpopular.

Here are some examples of ways in which teachers can set up a peer pressure strategy to reduce noise and maintain an orderly classroom. You might like to think about which would work best or be most appropriate for the class or classes which you teach.

" *Alright everyone. This is what's going to happen. You're going to work quietly with no shouting and no running around for ten minutes. I'm going to time you. And if you can do that, we're going to put some music on, and that music can stay on for the rest of the time while you finish the work IF and AS LONG AS you continue to work quietly. But – and this is very important – if EVEN ONE PERSON doesn't stick to that deal, there'll be no music for ANYONE. Is that clear? Any questions?*

" *Who would like us all to play a game for the last part of the lesson? Good! Well, that's what we'll do, but only if you can ALL get this work finished on time. That means working quietly and sensibly. And then we can have a game of* [whatever's appropriate to the class: eg Word Tennis/Hangman/Team Quiz/Pass the Answer etc.]. *But we won't be able to do that unless everyone has finished their work. Jordan and Ollie, that means you too.*

" *Okay everybody. Let's have some quiet now. I'm going to be giving you five minutes free chat time later on so you'll be able to finish your conversations and catch up with each other then. But you're going to have to earn it. If I see or hear anyone being noisy, disturbing other people, making it difficult for everyone to hear me or each other, then there'll be no free chat time for ANYONE. So I do hope **no one** is going to spoil the chance for everyone else.*

A Spot of Theory

In his book, Take Control of the Noisy Class *(2016),* Rob Plevin *suggests a variation on the peer pressure strategy which involves appointing a small number of learners to the role of 'Shushers'. At the teacher's signal, they all 'shush' the class from their various positions in the room. This introduces an element of fun into the strategy. (He suggests the possibility of providing them with some kind of badge of office – even special hats!) The underpinning theory here is partly neo-behaviourist – making noise control fun, and partly humanist – emphasising the importance of positive relationships for effective learning.*

Checklist

Use this to keep a record of what worked well for you and what didn't. A strategy that works with one class may not work so well with another. Keeping a checklist helps you to work out what factors or learner characteristics call for one approach rather than another. There's a line at the bottom for you to add your own most frequently used strategy, if it's not already included in the list.

Strategy	Tried it with...	On...(date)	It worked	It didn't work	Worth trying again?
1. Meet and greet*					
2. No time to chat					
3. Sparkle					
4. Pace					
5. All change					
6. Softly softly					
7. The silent wait					
8. Eyes front					
9. Mixing it up					
10. Back row seats					
11. Rewards					
12. Sanctions					
13. Peer pressure					
Your own strategy?					

DAY 5: They can't be bothered: combating boredom and disengagement

Why would learners be bored?

A bored learner is a potentially disruptive learner. And – more importantly – their disengagement will prevent them from gaining anything from the learning experience you're offering. There are many reasons why learners might be bored, and not all of these are the fault of the teacher. But it is nevertheless the teacher's responsibility to do something about it. This means it's important to be able to spot when learners are bored and – crucially – to be able to identify *why* they feel this way. Perhaps the work is too difficult and/or seems irrelevant to them; perhaps it's too easy and doesn't offer them sufficient challenge; or it may be that they're restless, in need of a break or a change of activity. It could even be something to do with the way you've planned or presented the lesson. The following strategies offer you ways of preventing or combating learners' boredom and encouraging a positive engagement with learning.

Today's strategies

- Is it you? Lesson planning for maximum engagement:
  1. Attention!
  2. Keeping up the pace

- Positive starts and endings to lessons:
  3. Sock it to them
  4. Up to the wire

- All change – surprise them:
  5. Your move
  6. Boldly go
  7. Surprise, surprise!

- Less teaching, more learning:
  8. Action stations
  9. Talk less, listen more

- Say it again or say it differently:
  10. Put it another way
  11. Over and over

- Creating situations where praise can be earned and given:
  12. Good try
  13. Leading roles

- Turning the tables (keeping an eye on seating):
  14. New neighbours
  15. Moving day

Strategy: Is it you? Lesson planning for maximum engagement

If learners seem bored or too easily distracted and reluctant to engage, it may be that you'll need to re-think the planning of your lesson to take further into account the characteristics of these particular learners: their age, their degree of restlessness, their natural attention span, and so on. It may be that you're expecting the impossible – that they'll sit and listen silently for 20 minutes, for example; or work quietly in pairs without chatter. It's only by careful observation and by trial and error that you'll work out where your planning is going wrong. Here are some things you can try:

1. Attention!

Because attention spans vary, it's useful to build in frequent changes of learner activity and observe what timings seem to work best for the class as a whole. If you find, for instance, that a change of activity or focus every ten minutes or so succeeds in keeping the attention and interest of most of the class, you can provide differentiated activities for the few whose attention span is shorter and who will therefore respond better to more frequent change and shorter tasks. On the other hand, it may be that the strategy of ten minutes per task or activity keeps everybody on board. You won't know until you try.

2. Keeping up the pace

When setting tasks, keep timings tight and give regular updates on how much time is left. Keeping up the lesson pace like this lends a sense of urgency, excitement and competition, which learners often respond to positively. Regular reminders that time is ticking is a great antidote to boredom. It creates a similar atmosphere to a competitive sporting event – something that many learners feel comfortable, familiar and positive with.

Spotting signs of boredom

Think of a recent lesson where you experienced difficulty with learners becoming disengaged or disruptive. Look carefully at your plan for that lesson.

- How long were learners expected to engage with any one task or activity (for example, listening to you, carrying out a task in small groups, working individually)?

- How frequently did you give them a change of task, activity or focus?

- How clearly did you provide a countdown of the time remaining for each task/activity?

- How tightly did you keep the timings?

- At what point(s) in the lesson was the disengagement or disruption at its worst?

Is there anything you can learn from this for future planning?

On an interest scale Sir, we are at minus two

Strategy: Positive starts and endings to lessons

The idea here is to grab learners' attention from the outset of the lesson, and keep it from fizzling out as the lesson approaches its end. The beginning and end are the two 'danger' points. If you don't engage learners from the start, the lesson will become one long struggle to get them on board. And if they're already chatting and putting their things away before the end of the lesson, you lose valuable learning time. Here are some ways to avoid this.

3. Sock it to them

To get everyone interested right from the word go, have the learners draw lots (like a raffle), where the winner is given a choice over some element of the lesson. For example, you could allow them to choose from a list of starter activities, or background music, or some other component of the lesson about which you feel there can be some flexibility. This not only introduces the elements of fun and choice, but also stresses the idea that learners – not just teachers – have ownership over the lesson. (This has been done successfully using raffle tickets drawn from a sock – hence the name!)

4. Up to the wire

Try withholding the answers to a quiz or similar competitive activity, held earlier in the lesson, until the very end; at which point you will give out the 'prizes' or announce the awards – whether these are sweets, stars, team points, or key roles for the next lesson. Alternatively, you can use the whole quiz/competition for a finishing activity. The key here is to keep the class interested right to the very end of the lesson.

Here is a teacher combining both strategies in order to engage the class's interest from the outset and maintain it even in the closing minutes of the lesson.

" As the teacher welcomes the learners into the room she gets each of them to take a raffle ticket out of a giant Christmas sock. *'Sit down quickly and settle down,'* she says. *'Settle down and listen carefully because I'm going to read out the winning number. Have you all got your tickets in front of you? Jaden? Where's yours?'*

" *'I dropped it,'* says Jaden.

" *'Already?'* says the teacher. *'Well that's a shame. If you've lost it, you won't be able to win, will you? Next time, keep it safe. Okay, the rest of you. Listen carefully. The winning number is… Number 23.'*

" A boy near the back of the room squeals and raises his hand. *'Yes!'* he shouts. *'It's me!'*

" The teacher leads the class in a round of applause. *'Okay,'* she says. *'So you get the choice today, Jack. Which of our starter activities are you going to choose for us?'*

" *'A quiz,'* says Jack. *'But different teams from yesterday.'*

" *'A quiz it is,'* says the teacher. *'But today I'm not going to give the answers until later on, near the end of the lesson. So we'll have to wait a bit today to see which team's the winner this time.'*

Questions:

★ How well did the teacher deal with Jaden's lost ticket? Would you have dealt with it differently; and if so, how and why?

★ If you were the teacher, what strategy might you use to divide the class into *'different teams from yesterday'*?

★ In practical terms, what choices could you offer your class (or classes) as a prize?

★ If you were using this strategy, what signs would you look out for to evaluate whether it was working effectively?

★ What would you do if the same learner had the winning number two days in a row?

★ How would you evaluate whether this strategy would be appropriate for a specific class? In your view, what would constitute valid reasons not to use it?

Strategy: All change – surprise them

It's all too easy for lessons to get into a rut. You may have a preferred style of teaching or a few favourite resources that you feel comfortable and confident with. You may always stand in the same place when you're talking to the class, or always employ the same strategies so that learners always know what's coming: groupwork, for example, or worksheets. It's certainly true that the use of familiar routines can give learners – particularly younger pupils – a sense of safety and security. But too much routine can have its downside too, because it has the potential to become boring and uninspiring. That's when learners switch off.

5. Your move

Keep on the move. Don't always stand on one spot when you're talking to the class. Or perhaps you do already walk about – in which case, don't always pace the same old route, between your table and the window, or whatever it may be, like a polar bear behind bars. Don't have routine routes and moves. Be unpredictable. That way you'll keep learners' attention.

6. Boldly go

Do something unfamiliar. Extend your repertoire of strategies or resources. Learn to use some available technology or other resource which you may have avoided using up to now. Make yourself familiar with it so that you feel comfortable and confident about incorporating it into lessons. Boldly go where you've not gone before. Wake your learners up with something they're not expecting.

7. Surprise, surprise!

Find a new way to introduce a topic or activity, so that learners at first are not quite sure where it's going. Hook their interest and then surprise them. Instead of saying, *'Today we're going to talk about...'* whatever it's to be, try showing them a picture or a short YouTube clip or a relevant artefact and ask them to talk to you about it, or to ask you questions about it, or to guess what topic or activity it's leading up to. This is designed to hook their interest and draw them in, just as the opening shots of a good film will grab the attention of the audience and get them intrigued to know what's going to happen next.

● Next time you're in the classroom, be mindful of where you position yourself. Notice where you sit or stand, how much you move about the room and what routes you take. Do you have a favourite 'spot' to stand, a favourite route where you pace back and forth? Once you become aware of these habits you can begin to break them, become less predictable and more likely to hold learners' attention.

● Choose one resource or teaching method which you have so far avoided using because it puts you outside your comfort zone, and give it a go. Discover whether it wakes your learners up a bit.

● Next time you're introducing a new topic or activity, try incorporating a relevant image or artefact, rather than simply introducing it verbally.

Caution! Low flying teacher.

A Spot of Theory

Johann Pestalozzi (1746– 1827), founder of the Pestalozzi method of education, argued that children learn more effectively through activity and through handling and using material artefacts than solely through teacher talk.

Strategy: Less teaching, more learning

It's easy to assume that if there's lots of teaching going on in the classroom, there must also be lots of learning taking place, too. But of course we all know this isn't the case. You can talk as much or as entertainingly as you like, but if the learners aren't listening and taking it in there'll be no chance of learning outcomes being met. So it's important to ensure that they're working at least as hard as you are.

8. Action stations

When planning your lessons, make sure that learners are given the opportunity to engage actively with the subject or topic, rather than locking them into a passive role where all they are required to do is listen or respond. If they're being kept busy, they're less likely to be bored and more likely to be learning. Check your lesson plan over and see who's going to be doing most of the work. Learners need to be actively *doing* – otherwise how can you assess what they've learnt?

9. Talk less, listen more

Do you frequently find yourself telling your learners that they should be listening? It's important to remember that you should be listening, too. Effective assessment and useful evaluation are impossible unless we encourage learners to talk to us and listen carefully to what they say. Lessons should be a two-way conversation, never a monologue by the teacher. Try building in opportunities for learners to talk – to you and to each other – while you listen. This is structured, productive talk time; not the hubbub that tells you a class is bored or restless. And by showing them how to listen you are modelling the positive behaviour you would like to see from them.

Consider a recent lesson you have planned and taught in which learners seemed bored, disengaged or actively disruptive.

Draw a table of three columns (or use the one below) headed *Time, Teacher* and *Learner*. In the *Teacher* column, list all your activities during the lesson. In the *Learner* column, list all the learner activities. In the *Time* column, note down approximately how much time was spent on each activity.

In the partially completed example below there is a pattern of the teacher being active while the learners are mainly passive. This could account for learners becoming bored or disruptive.

✸ How does your own table compare?

✸ Does it suggest any changes you might usefully make when planning future lessons?

Time	Teacher	Learner
10 min	Talking, explaining	Listening
15 min	Demonstrating, showing	Watching
10 min	Asking questions	Answering questions

A Spot of Theory

'To put it bluntly, learning delivered primarily through teacher-talk is often the easiest option for both learners and teachers. It usually requires the least planning (assuming the teacher's subject knowledge is good) and it releases learners from an obligation to think, practise and explore.'

(Wallace, I and Kirkman, L (2014) *Talk-Less Teaching: Practice, Participation and Progress*. Carmarthen, Wales: Crown House)

Strategy: Say it again or say it differently

Learners can become bored and disengaged if they find they can't understand what you're trying to explain to them or what it is they're supposed to be doing. Sometimes you may know your subject so well – be so familiar with it, whether it's phonics, felt-making or French history – that it's easy to forget how complex it may seem to a learner, or how unfamiliar the vocabulary and terminology will be. If you think this might be the problem, here are some things you can try.

10. Put it another way

Make sure you always allow time to clarify, rephrase and to simplify. When you've explained something, explain it again using different words. Always define and explain words that may be unfamiliar to the learners. And then ask and invite questions so that you can assess whether further clarification may be needed. You may find the following mnemonic useful:

QRS (Question, Rephrase, Simplify)

11. Over and over

Be prepared to repeat explanations or instructions as often as necessary until you're sure that all learners have understood. It's important not to sigh, grow impatient, look or sound exasperated, or change your tone of voice in any way. Some learners will need to hear things several (or even many) times before they – and you – feel confident they have understood. It's important to accept this as part of their learning needs, and not penalise them for it by losing your patience with them. It's far better to repeat something several times than to have learners give up and become disruptive.

A Spot of Theory

A learner's active vocabulary is the range of words they are able to use accurately in their speech or writing. They will also possess a vocabulary of words which they recognise and comprehend but do not use. Therefore, learners' active vocabulary is usually more limited than their comprehension. This means that it is often difficult for a teacher to accurately predict what a learner will or will not easily understand. This is why rephrasing and simplification are so important.

Compare these two teachers' approaches to giving instructions. Who do you think is more in danger of causing frustration or losing the class's interest?

Teacher A:

" *I want you to draw a line down the right side of the paper. The right side! I said the right side! What are you drawing it down that side for, Ryan? I said the right side. And now another line across at a right angle. What do you mean, what's a right angle? You know what a right angle is. We've already done right angles. So draw it across at a right angle. Yasmin! What's that supposed to be? Is that supposed to be a right angle? That's not a right angle. I don't know what that is. And now I want you to join up those two corners. No! Frankie! What are you folding your paper up for? What are you doing? I said join those two corners with a line. Yes I did. That's what I said...*

Teacher B:

" *Let's see if we can remember our right from our left. Let's all wave our right hands. I'll just turn round so I'm facing the same way as you. Look at me or at other people if you're not sure. Keep your hands there. Okay, I'm turning back again now to have a look. Good. That's right, Ryan. It's your hand nearest the window. Good. Now I want you to draw a line all the way down that side of the paper, the right-hand side of the paper. Let's see. Good. Good. Now, do you remember what a right angle is? Who wants to show me on the board? That's right, Derren. Well done. So now I'd like you all to draw another line on your paper that crosses that first line at a right angle, like Derren has shown us on the board. It can be further up, like this. Or further down, like this. Wherever you like. But it needs to cross that first line at a right angle. Good. And now, you see these two places where your first line and your second line finish? Like this on the board? Either end of them. It doesn't matter. I'd like you to draw a straight line that joins one end of the first line to one end of the second line...*

You'll have noticed that Teacher A does repeat things a lot. But this only demonstrates the ineffectiveness of impatient repetition when no clarification or simplification are offered.

Strategy: Creating situations where praise can be earned and given

If it seems as though there's never any 'pay-off' for them, learners will lose interest and grow bored. There are two main sources of reward that a classroom can offer. The most important is the intrinsic reward to be gained from learning – the enjoyment and sense of achievement at learning something new. The other is reward in terms of praise from the teacher. Sadly, it's usually the learners that gain the first of these who also gain the second. The others are left wondering what's in it for them. So it's important to create opportunities to praise those who are struggling to find satisfaction in the actual process of learning, so that they don't lose interest in it altogether.

12. Good try

Experiment with praising for effort rather than for achievement. Try it for one lesson and see what happens. Those learners who habitually achieve well will obviously have made an effort, so they won't be missing out. But try to word your praise so that it focuses on how hard they have worked rather than on the finished task. Learners who believe they have no hope of being praised for what they can do will begin to notice that praise can also be won for trying. Wherever you see them make the slightest effort – even if it's only to stop talking for a minute and pick up their pencil – use that as an opportunity to praise them for it. Praise is addictive. They'll want more. This makes it a very effective way of getting people to re-engage with learning.

13. Leading roles

You can also create opportunities to give praise to potentially disruptive learners by giving them a role in the lesson which you know they'll enjoy and can be praised for. This could be anything that gets them involved, from chief cleaner of the whiteboard to observer or messenger in small group work; from referee in a class competition to hander out of worksheets or the person who makes sure all the computer monitors are turned off at the end of the lesson. Draw them in, provide them with an opportunity to contribute, and praise them for putting the effort in.

Strategy in action

Think of three learners you work with who appear bored, show little interest and are sometimes disruptive in lessons. Now make two lists:

A. Manageable roles you could allocate to them for the next lesson which might create the opportunity for you to give them some praise.

B. Signs of effort that you would be prepared to praise, for example:

- stopping talking when you ask them to;
- picking up their pencil;
- contributing something – however minor – to a class or group discussion;
- paying attention to you while you're speaking to the class;
- writing a few words/a few lines;
- helping a classmate with a learning task.

Try some of these out in practice at the next opportunity and make a note of what seemed to work and might be worth using again.

A Spot of Theory

A learner's lack of belief in their own ability or intelligence can limit their potential to learn. The American psychologist Carol Dweck refers to this as fixed mindset. *She suggests that we should try to help learners develop a* growth mindset, *which is the belief that ability can be developed through hard work. This is where praise for effort plays an important role.*

Dweck, C (2012) Mindset: How You Can Fulfil Your Potential. *London: Robinson.*

Strategy: Turning the tables (keeping an eye on seating)

Are learners always looking at you from the same angle? Are they always working next to the same people, with the same view of the same posters or the back of someone's head? Is it always the same-old-same-old? This could be one reason some of them get bored. Shake them up a bit. Try this:

14. New neighbours

Seat everyone differently. Make this fun by getting them to draw their seating allocation out of a hat; or make it into a game by giving instructions such as, *'Find a seat next to someone whose birthday is in the same month as yours/who has different coloured eyes to yours/whose name contains two of the same letters of the alphabet as yours'*. (Use your ingenuity to pair up those who may be left over.) As well as introducing a bit of fun and giving learners a new view of things, New Neighbours has the added advantage of separating pairs or small groups who habitually distract one another or encourage one another to be disruptive.

15. Moving day

Instead of moving the learners around, rearrange their tables or desks into a different configuration – from rows to a boardroom arrangement; from small groups to rows; from large table groupings to small. Or move your own desk or habitual teaching position to the other end of the classroom, or to the side. Or do both these things. A new look to the teaching environment will wake everyone up and has the potential to jolt learners out of their assumed manner of boredom or disinterest. The signal you're sending here is: New look – new start.

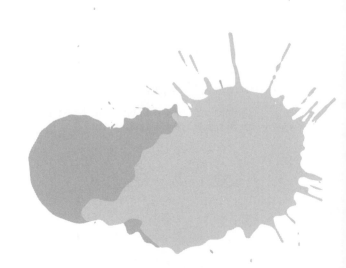

Here is one teacher's experience.

" I was having trouble with a large class because only about half of them were paying attention. The other half were lounging about. They weren't being disruptive exactly, but they weren't doing any work and they weren't listening, and I think that was undermining the motivation of the others. It just got harder and harder.

And then my mentor suggested that I try rearranging the classroom. How it was at this point, they were sitting at small groups of tables, some of them half turned away from me and the groups at the back were doing their own thing and were difficult for me to make any eye contact with.

So I decided to take my mentor's advice and move things round a bit. I got in early and asked the caretaker to help me. We arranged all the tables in one big horseshoe shape with the open end facing me, my table and the whiteboard. It meant that we would all be able to see each other, they could all see me, and no one could easily opt out of what we were doing because everyone would notice.

When they came in you would have thought I'd set up a circus with a big top in there. There was so much ooh-ing and aah-ing and talking about it. But once they got sat down and the lesson got started, things were SO different.

The communication both ways felt so much easier. Kids joined in who'd never joined in my lessons properly before. The new arrangement allows me to talk face-to-face with every individual and give one-to-one help where necessary. I can walk around the inside of that horseshoe shape and have a quiet word with any one of them. And they know it! It's really been worth the initial hassle.

And I guess I have our caretaker to thank, too. If she'd been less obliging it would have been really difficult to organise.

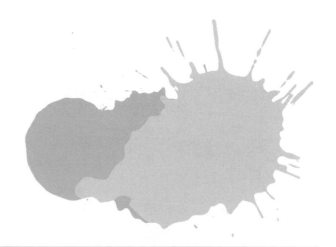

Checklist

Use this to keep a record
of what worked well for
you and what didn't.
A strategy that works with
one class may not work so
well with another. Keeping
a checklist helps you to
work out what factors or
learner characteristics call
for one approach rather
than another. There's a
line at the bottom for you
to add your own most
frequently used strategy, if
it's not already included in
the list.

Strategy	Tried it with...	On (date)	It worked	It didn't work	Worth trying again?
1. Attention!					
2. Keeping up the pace					
3. Sock it to them					
4. Up to the wire					
5. Your move					
6. Boldly go					
7. Surprise, surprise!					
8. Action stations					
9. Talk less, listen more					
10. Put it another way					
11. Over and over					
12. Good try*					
13. Leading roles					
14. New neighbours					
15. Moving day					
Your own strategy?					

DAY 6: Who's the boss?: disarming ringleaders and attention seekers

Being in charge

It's important to your learners' sense of security that you should be seen to be safely in charge of what's going on in the classroom. A disruptive or non-compliant learner can too easily distract the attention of the class from where it ought to be – on their learning; and you will need to ensure that you don't provide them with the platform to do that. This chapter provides you with useful strategies for downplaying, defusing and disarming potentially disruptive behaviour and dealing with situations where a learner – or group of learners – is competing for the class's attention or demanding a disruptive level of attention from you.

Being in charge

Strategy: Keeping the spotlight where you want it

You don't always have to be in the spotlight. You'll often want your learners to listen to each other, give feedback to one another, and to show or demonstrate their good work. So there's nothing wrong with handing over the spotlight to a learner, as long as it's for the right reason. But when you're addressing behaviour issues it's very important to avoid your behaviour management strategies becoming an entertaining floor show for the rest of the class. The last thing you want to do is to hand over the spotlight to a non-compliant or confrontational learner and allow them to star in their own drama of *Me versus the Teacher*. If you give them the spotlight, you're rewarding their bad behaviour. And if you reward it like that, you'll simply reinforce it.

1. No dramas

To keep the class's attention where it should be – on their learning – always keep in mind this four-point plan:

* You should keep your interventions low-key where possible and where appropriate.

* If the intervention has to be highly visible, make sure you're not providing the culprit with the starring role.

* Don't make interventions as a knee-jerk reaction. To remain in control, you need first to be in control of *yourself*.

* When addressing a behaviour problem you should be seen by the learners as proactive, not reactive. If learners are seen to be 'pulling your strings' by their behaviour, this shows that it's they – not you – who are in control.

Some of the strategies we've looked at previously (for example, on Day 3) can also be very useful in keeping the spotlight where you want it and preventing the negative behaviour of an individual or group becoming the focus of the class's attention. These include most importantly:

* tactical ignoring (page 34);

* assumption of compliance (page 36);

* avoiding giving direct orders (page 38).

Karl is repeatedly kicking his neighbour's chair. In which of the following scenarios is the teacher most likely to remain in control of the situation, and in which ones is the teacher in danger of drawing the whole class's attention to what's going on and handing over the spotlight to the learner?

A. The teacher walks over to Karl and says quietly, *'Karl, you're kicking Lily's chair. I'd like you to sit properly and get on with your work.'* The teacher walks away.

B. The teacher walks over to Karl and says quietly, *'Karl, you're kicking Lily's chair. I'd like you to sit properly and get on with your work.'* The teacher stands there and waits.

C. The teacher walks over to Karl and says loudly, *'Karl! Stop it and get on with what you're supposed to be doing.'* The teacher stands there and waits.

D. The teacher shouts from the front, *'Karl! What are you doing?'* Karl shouts back, *'Kicking Lily's chair, isn't it?'* The class laugh.

E. The teacher says from the front, *'Karl, I'd like you to stop that now and let Lily get on with her work.'* After a few minutes, the teacher tries again: *'Karl. I've told you once. Stop kicking the chair.'* And then a few minutes later, *'Karl! What have I told you?'* Karl gives the chair another kick and says, *'Stop kicking the chair?'*

A Spot of Theory

Wallace and Kirkman's Talk-Less Teaching (Crown House, 2014) reminds us that although you need to keep control of where the spotlight shines, it doesn't always have to shine on you. Classes who are encouraged to get involved actively with their learning, discussing it and listening to each other, are less likely to engage in disruptive behaviour than those who are expected to simply sit and listen.

Strategy: Allocating 'empowering' roles

If you're planning a learning activity involving small groups or the whole class working as one large group, you can forestall problems by building in specific roles for the learners who are otherwise most likely to cause disruption. As we've already seen in Days 1 to 5, disruptive learners are often behaving that way because they want attention or because they want to avoid doing work they're scared is too difficult for them.

2. Power to the people i

Planning ahead and allocating learners a role – such as Observer, Group Messenger, Spokesperson or Peace-keeper – can make them feel they are being valued and at the same time allows them a role which doesn't put them in direct competition with any other learner. This way they learn they can get attention for doing something positive and can get actively involved in a learning activity without fear of failure. This strategy also has the added advantage of introducing reluctant learners to the idea that learning can be fun and can build – not undermine – their self-esteem. If you and your class have negotiated a set of rules for classroom behaviour, you can appoint a potentially non-compliant learner to be one of those who monitors whether the rules are being adhered to. It's surprising how concerned with compliance a previously difficult learner can become when given such a role.

3. Power to the people ii

Allocating an empowering role can also be a spontaneous strategy in response to a particular situation. For example: *'I'd like you to stop doing that, Brianna, and give these worksheets out for me, please.'* Or, *'You're making a lot of noise, Bif. We're going to take a vote in a minute and I'd like you to count hands for me.'*

If you're worried that this might look like rewarding bad behaviour, remember that what you're doing is encouraging the learner to earn attention by doing something positive and helpful. And you're giving them the opportunity to get some praise and discover how good that feels.

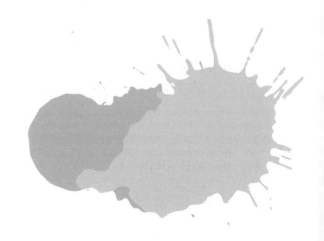

In the following scenarios, think about what sort of empowering roles the teacher could allocate which would have a good chance of addressing the problem behaviour.

A. The class has been divided into small groups and asked to come up with ideas. One learner isn't contributing anything to his group. Instead he's trying to distract his friend who's sitting with another group by calling across to him and tipping his chair back in an effort to reach for something to throw at him. The teacher needs to think on his feet. What role could he give this learner?

B. The whole class is having a discussion led by the teacher. Three girls sitting at one table are talking loudly about something else and refusing to join in. What role or roles could the teacher give them immediately to get them involved? What roles could the teacher plan in advance to allocate to them next time there's a whole-class discussion?

C. Reece has a reputation for being noisy and rude. He likes making the rest of the class laugh. The teacher is looking over the plan for the next day's lesson. What sort of role could he create for Reece which would harness his energy and get him working with, not against, the teacher?

A Spot of Theory

As we've seen in previous chapters, praise can work well as a reward for positive behaviour – but we can only use it if someone deserves it. The strategy of allocating a role creates an opportunity for you as the teacher to justifiably give praise to a learner who might normally never receive any. This is a useful first step in behaviour management by positive reinforcement.

Strategy: Using and avoiding eye contact

Eye contact is a very powerful tool in the classroom. It can be used to encourage, to praise, to warn, to put learners at ease or to keep them on their toes. So it's important that, wherever possible, the classroom seating should be arranged in a way that allows you to make eye contact with every learner. Where classrooms are routinely arranged to seat groups of learners around tables, you'll have to move around the room in order to ensure you make eye contact with everyone. If you find there are learners who habitually choose a seat that puts their back to you, it may be that they're hoping to avoid making eye contact with you, keeping a low profile in case, for example, you challenge their behaviour or ask them a question they can't answer.

4. Eye to eye

If a small group or clique is causing disruption, there is often the temptation to either ignore them or give them stony looks. A more effective tactic is to use positive eye contact as a reward whenever there is any sign of one or more of them paying attention. Friendly, smiling eye contact is surprisingly powerful when used as a reward. Learners who have become used to teachers frowning at them in disapproval may be surprised by the feel-good factor, and want more. Disruptive learners may be opting out because they assume they would never win your approval. Using positive eye contact to draw them in and make them feel included can be surprisingly effective.

5. Eyes down

Avoiding eye contact with a learner can be a useful strategy, but only in very specific scenarios where an individual or small group are monopolising class time with their questions or over-long answers or interminable presentation, to the point where you can see that the rest of the class has lost interest and you need to take charge of what's happening. Temporarily withdrawing eye contact in situations like this will discourage that individual or individuals from taking up more floor time. But *temporarily* is the operative word here.

Imagine you are carrying out a peer observation on a colleague. This is what you see.

As the teacher begins the lesson you can see at once that most of the class is paying close attention but that there are three girls sitting near the window who are talking between themselves. The table arrangement means that two of them are half turned away from the teacher and the third has her back turned entirely. The teacher sits at his own table and asks some questions to see what learners have remembered from their previous lesson. The keen ones listen and respond. The most responsive learners are sitting at the side of the room furthest from the window. The teacher begins to concentrate his attention there, making very little eye contact with the other side of the room and none at all with the three girls who are talking. Gradually, the learners he is ignoring all begin to lose interest. At one point, the girl sitting with her back to the teacher turns in her chair and asks the teacher a question. *'I've explained that already,'* says the teacher, barely glancing at her. The girl resumes her chat with her friends. The teacher sets the learners off on a task. He then has a long conversation with one of the keen learners, who monopolises his attention for much of the rest of the lesson, so much so that he doesn't notice when the learners on the other side of the classroom raise their hands to ask him something.

At the end of the lesson he says to you,

" *It's a difficult class. There's such a wide range of learners. Some just aren't interested.*

⬥ What do you think he gets wrong here?

⬥ What advice would you give him about eye contact and how to use it?

⬥ If you were teaching this class, how would you have dealt with:
  ⬥ the seating arrangement;
  ⬥ the girls who are talking;
  ⬥ the keen learner;
  ⬥ the apparent divide between responsive learners on one side of the room and less engaged readers on the other?

⬥ If you were teaching this class, would you have sat at the teacher's table? If not, what would you have done instead, and why?

Strategy: Disbanding cliques and dispersing followers

One of the most difficult classroom situations to deal with is when you are faced with a disruptive group of learners, often led by a particular ringleader who sometimes seems to have more real power in the classroom than you do. Don't worry! There are several strategies which can be very effective in this situation.

6. Divide and rule

What you really want to do is to disperse a disruptive group. While just telling them to split up and move may get a point-blank refusal, you can incorporate into your lesson planning some ways of reshuffling the class that are difficult for them to resist. For example:

* Plan activities using teams. Either draw names out of a hat, or have two or more non-disruptive learners pick their teams.

* Plan small group work where the groups are formed by counting off around the class, as we've seen before: *one*, *two*, *three*, *four*, *five* – all the ones get in a group; all the twos get in a group, etc. You should do the numbering off briskly. The dispersal looks random, and has the advantage of novelty.

* Plan small group work where one learner from each group moves on to share ideas with the next group whenever you give a signal (whistle, bell, handclap) every few minutes. It must be a different learner each time. This effectively breaks up cliques who have elected to work together.

7. Recruit the leader

Give the ringleader a task or role that separates him or her from their group. A good choice of role is one that could be classified as your 'helper': giving out worksheets, counting hands, collating class answers on a whiteboard or smartboard. This shifts the whole dynamic, making you and the erstwhile ringleader a team and leaving his old 'team' leaderless.

8. Peer pressure – again!

We've already talked a lot about using peer pressure; and it is a particularly useful strategy when faced with the problem of disruptive groups and their ringleaders. Remember: this strategy works by changing the classroom dynamic so that instead of it being: You (teacher) versus Them (learners), it becomes instead: Us (the teacher and class combined) versus Him/Her (the non-compliant learner), like this:

$$\text{You versus them} \longrightarrow \text{Us versus him/her}$$

You can use this approach to drive a wedge between a ringleader and his or her followers through the use of rewards (have a look again at Day 4 for some ideas about rewards). Even learners who appear immune to teacher disapproval will often be reluctant to be on the receiving end of disapproval from their classmates for making them lose out on a reward that most of them have worked hard for.

I recently observed a teacher using all three of these strategies. Look at the way she combines them.

The teacher says:

> *Okay everyone. We're going to do some work in teams today and if you can get into your teams nice and quickly with no fuss, we'll have some music on while you're working. Ready? Are you listening? I'm going to count round the class. I'm going to give each of you a number. You need to remember it carefully, and then I'm going to ask you to get in a group with others who have the same number as you. Ready? Remember – if you can do this sensibly we'll have some music on. Listen to see what number you are: one, two, three or four. Because we're going to have four groups. Here we go.*

The teacher points to each learner in turn, numbering them off.

> *One, two, three, four, one, two, three four ...*

By this process a disruptive group of four who are sitting together are each allocated a different number. The ringleader, Josh, begins to object.

The teacher breaks off her counting for a moment to say,

> *Oh, Josh, I need your help please. Could you watch the counting carefully and check that people are going where they're told? Let's make sure we earn the music. Thank you.*

Leaving no room for objections or a reply, she carries on counting:

> *One, two, three ...*

Questions:

- Why do you think this approach worked so well?
- Is it an approach that could work for you and your classes?

What would you do?

Within your class of 30 learners, two close groups or cliques have formed, one of five girls and one of six boys. These two groups are both noisy and unco-operative and you've noticed that their behaviour is beginning to disrupt the learning of the rest of the class. You decide that it's got to the point where you must do something about it.

- Which strategy or strategies would you try first, and why?

Strategy: Winning hearts and minds

While it's important to remember that your relationship with your class is as a teacher, not as a friend, a positive friendly approach is one of the most effective ways to disarm negative or disruptive learners. Being cheerful, friendly and positive does not mean you are being 'soft'. It's a way of making learners feel more positive about themselves and about being there in the classroom. We know that disruption or refusal to comply can be an indication that the learner doesn't feel able or confident enough to engage with the lesson. Messing about instead can be an act of bravado to cover their underlying fear – of school, of failure, of you.

An angry or hostile response from you can reinforce their negative mindset and simply make the problem worse. So here are two strategies for building mutual respect and establishing a positive working relationship.

9. Naming names

Use learners' names at every opportunity. It shows you acknowledge them as individuals and reinforces your one-to-one relationship with each of them. Don't name names only when you're telling someone off. If you teach many different classes you'll probably need to make a special effort to learn names. Do this as early on as possible. And make sure everyone in the class knows each other's names too. Apart from name badges and seating plans, there are several useful activities which will help with this. For example:

* As part of a question and answer activity, point with both hands to the learner you want to answer the question. That learner should say their name, answer, and then point with both hands to the learner they choose to answer the next question. That learner says their name and answers your next question, and so on. (Keep the questions easy for this so that no one feels threatened.)

* Working in pairs, learners 'interview' their partner for one minute each and then introduce them to the rest of the class by name, saying a few words about them.

10. Caring and sharing

At the beginning of the lesson, give each learner the name of a classmate on a folded piece of paper. They must not show this to anyone else. (If you have an odd number you can join in this yourself.) Their brief is that they should secretly observe their named classmate during the lesson and then write down something they think they deserve praise for. This will be easier in some cases than others! But this emphasis on the positive – and the encouragement to actively look for behaviour that can be rewarded by praise – works by (1) holding up examples of positive behaviour and (2) giving even difficult learners a taste for praise and some good ideas about how to earn it.

Next time you are observed teaching, ask the observer to look particularly at how you use (or don't use) learners' names. If you have no observations coming up soon, make a particular point of noticing this for yourself. Some questions you'll find useful to ask yourself are:

- Do you use names positively (*'Well done, Sean. That looks really good!'*), or only when you're telling someone off? (*'Sean! Don't do that!'*)

- Do you sometimes dispense with names and use general phrases such as, *you lot; front table; you over there*?

- Do you know *everyone's* name? Are there learners you avoid addressing because you're not sure?

- Are you pronouncing everyone's name correctly? Don't be afraid to check this with the learner if their name is one that's unfamiliar to you.

- Do you overuse some names? This could be a sign that you're paying too much attention to some individuals and not enough to others. Or that there are some you've not learnt yet.

A Spot of Theory

Research has shown that there are fewer incidents of disruptive behaviour in classes where the teacher looks cheerful, appears enthusiastic about what they're teaching, demonstrates a sense of humour and is perceived by the learners as friendly and approachable.

Wallace, S (2014) When You're Smiling: Exploring How Teachers Motivate and Engage Learners in the Further Education Sector. Journal of Further and Higher Education, *38(3): 346–60.*

Checklist

Use this to keep a record
of what worked well for
you and what didn't.
A strategy that works with
one class may not work so
well with another. Keeping
a checklist helps you to
work out what factors or
learner characteristics call
for one approach rather
than another. There's a
line at the bottom for you
to add your own most
frequently used strategy, if
it's not already included in
the list.

Strategy	Tried it with...	On (date)	It worked	It didn't work	Worth trying again?
1. No dramas					
2. Power to the people i					
3. Power to the people ii*					
4. Eye to eye					
5. Eyes down					
6. Divide and rule					
7. Recruit the leader					
8. Peer pressure – again!					
9. Naming names					
10. Caring and sharing					
Your own strategy?					

DAY 7: You can do this: managing your own fears and anxieties

Keeping calm and thinking clearly

The strategies suggested in this final chapter are general ones, designed to keep you calm and grounded when you're dealing day to day with difficult classroom situations. They are about surviving to teach another day; holding on to your enthusiasm in the face of challenging situations; and drawing on your inner strength and resourcefulness. It's all too easy to become anxious when you're wondering whether yesterday's difficult class is going to be even more disruptive tomorrow. Anxiety can be disabling, causing you to fear the worst and sapping your confidence in yourself as a teacher. Here are some simple ways you can begin to build up your confidence and enthusiasm so that you can enjoy the experience of being a teacher – one of the most rewarding professions you could choose.

- ✹ Demonstrating a sense of humour:
    1. Laugh and the world laughs with you ...
    2. They who laugh first ...
- ✹ Maintaining self-control:
    3. The mask
    4. Respond, don't react
- ✹ Remember that most disengaged behaviour arises from fear:
    5. Feel the fear
- ✹ Happy to know you:
    6. Smile
    7. Look-a-like
- ✹ Breathing and mindfulness:
    8. Breathe stress away
    9. Mindfulness
- ✹ Making the most of your position:
    10. Your advantage
- ✹ Keeping it all in perspective:
    11. Nothing personal

Strategy: Demonstrating a sense of humour

Sometimes all it takes is to be able to laugh along with the class. If they're laughing and you're scowling disapprovingly, you've immediately created a polarisation, a 'you versus them' situation. Some laughter, of course, is not permissible – laughter derived from racism, sexism or any other type of bullying – and must be dealt with swiftly and rigorously. But most often laughter among the young is based on high spirits and is a positive thing. If you and your learners can make each other laugh, you'll feel more positive about working together.

1. Laugh and the world laughs with you...

Relatively harmless laughter – even if it's causing some low-level disruption to your lesson – is more easily handled if you can smile tolerantly or even join in. Getting cross and trying to shut it down can often just cause it to escalate, and your obvious disapproval makes you 'the enemy'. This only adds to your negative feelings or sense of failure. When you laugh, you feel better. Discouraging laughter in the classroom is a battle you don't have to fight. Save your energy. Relax, and laugh along with the learners sometimes.

2. They who laugh first...

Try leading the laughter sometimes. Laugh at yourself. A teacher who stands too much on their own dignity makes a very tempting target, so don't be afraid to make a joke of your own mistakes, or your dress sense, or your ignorance about Pokémon Go, or whatever it is that will amuse the class and have them laughing along with you. Or you can demonstrate you have a sense of humour by using visual jokes – cartoons, YouTube clips, captioned photos – when you design your resources. Experiment and see what gets a laugh. They'll begin to discover you have a sense of humour and you'll be learning more about theirs.

Here are some things you should do and some things you should avoid when it comes to demonstrating a sense of humour in the classroom.

Do	Don't
Do be prepared to laugh at yourself.	Don't tell jokes. However funny they sounded on TV last night, they could just fall flat when you tell them, and then you'll feel embarrassed.
Do be prepared to laugh along with learners (unless their laughter is inappropriate or cruel).	Don't raise laughter by mocking learners who are easy targets. The only person you should mock is yourself.
Do use humour – such as cartoons – to illustrate slides and handouts.	Don't be cruel. Cruel laughter has no place in the classroom. You should always remember that one of your key roles is to model appropriate behaviour for your learners.
Do challenge and reprimand learners whose laughter expresses mockery or cruelty or bullying of any kind.	Don't cause offence by raising a laugh at the expense of minority groups or people's political or religious beliefs.
Do admit it if you don't get the joke.	Don't laugh along regardless just to look cool - you might be in tricky territory.
Do demonstrate a professional attitude	Don't ever join in laughter at a colleague's expense
in relation to colleagues.	

Strategy: Maintaining self-control

The key to 'controlling' a class is to first be able to control yourself. If you are in control of yourself, you won't get that feeling of being at the mercy of the class or that your chances of success as a teacher are dependent on the learners' unpredictable moods and behaviour. When you exert self-control you feel more confident and empowered. Here are some ways to start.

3. The mask

When you are in the classroom, think of yourself as an actor on a stage. The role you are playing is that of 'The Teacher'. In Greek drama, each actor wore a mask to indicate which character they were playing. This was called the *persona*. Think of yourself as wearing the *persona* of 'The Teacher'. This is a role in which you are required to be a model of controlled adult behaviour. It is a strong role – the role of someone who is in charge. As 'The Teacher', you feel more empowered and less vulnerable than you would if you were not in this role. Being mindful of the role you play can give you the distance and control to play it with confidence. (But if you find yourself actually wearing a mask, you've taken this too far!)

4. Respond, don't react

When things are going badly in the classroom – and particularly when you're faced with disruptive behaviour – there's a natural tendency to *react* in a kneejerk way. This may lead to you shouting, saying the wrong thing, or getting upset – all reactions which may well cause the problem to escalate. The answer here is to take a breath and then *respond* rather than react. The two are very different. When you react, it is the learner who is pulling your strings. But when you respond, you are taking control of what you say or do. A response is something you have thought out, reflected on, given

some consideration to, even if only for a few seconds. This reflection time, however brief, is what is missing when you simply react. To react is to act without thinking. This is why it often goes so badly wrong.

Reacting

Incident

↓

Teacher Reaction (eg angry shouting)

Responding

Incident

↓

Reflection (eg *'If I shout I'll make things worse'*)

↓

Teacher Response (eg speaks quietly)

A Spot of Theory

In writing about behaviour management, Paul Dix emphasises the point that, as teachers, the behaviour we must control is our own. Responding instead of reacting is a part of this self-control

In the following alternative versions of the same incidents:

⬤ Which teacher is reacting and which is responding?

⬤ Which teacher appears more in control?

⬤ Which teacher is building positive relationships with the learners?

⬤ Which teacher is supporting learning most effectively?

1	Learner: *'I'm not doing this. I hate reading.'*	Teacher A: *'Stop moaning and get on with it.'*
		Teacher B: *'Oh? Why's that?'*
2	Learner: *'If she pushes me again I'm going to punch her.'*	Teacher A: *'Right! That's it! You're both in isolation.'*
		Teacher B: *'Why don't you both tell me what this is about? Otherwise there's a danger I'm going to have put you both in isolation.'*
3	Learner: *'This is so f...ing boring.'*	Teacher A: *'Right! Get out! I've told you before. I'll have no swearing in this classroom.'*
		Teacher B: *'You're bored? Okay, come on, tell me why. What's up? But without swearing, please.'*
4	The learner is running about the classroom and won't stay in his seat.	Teacher A: *'Oy! Sit down! That's it. I've had enough of you. Running around like a little rodent. You can spend the rest of the day with Ms [Scary Headteacher].'*
		Teacher B: *'I'm going to count to ten, Ivan. And if you're not sitting down nicely by then I'll have to ask Ms [Scary Headteacher] to take you to her office. And you'll miss your break. We don't want that, do we?'*

Strategy: Remember that most disengaged behaviour arises from fear

5. Feel the fear

You may be feeling anxious about facing the badly behaved class, but it will help you if you remind yourself that beneath all the noise and bluster they are probably feeling much more anxious than you are. As we've seen before, a lot of disengaged or disruptive behaviour arises from fear. Try to think of such behaviour as fear in disguise. This will help you to gain some distance and be able to see that it may not be a reflection on you or your teaching but rather a puzzle to unpick: What is it they're afraid of? How can you help allay that fear? This is part of what it means to be a professional: being able to step back, analyse, and come back with possible solutions until you find out what works. Asking learners directly, *'What are you afraid of?'* or, *'What's worrying you?'* will sometimes work, but needs to be approached with caution. Some would see this as a challenge, or even an insult, and would probably deny feeling any fear at all. And – in one way – that might be true, because the fear that drives their behaviour may well be unconscious fear that they cannot acknowledge, even to themselves.

A Spot of Theory

Many psychologists, and psychotherapists such as Thom Rutledge (Embracing Fear, 2002) tell us that fear underlies most – if not all – negative emotions and problem behaviours.

Here are some examples of problem behaviour.

Highlight those you think might be driven by fear.

- Throwing books on the floor
- Staring out of the window instead of working
- Hitting or kicking other learners
- Folding their arms and refusing to do a task
- Running around and refusing to sit down
- Having a 'meltdown' – shouting and swearing
- Refusing to share with other learners
- Talking loudly while you're talking
- Answering you back
- Taking things from other learners
- Often arriving late
- Not handing in homework
- Defacing or destroying learning materials

Answer

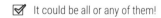 It could be all or any of them!

Strategy: Happy to know you

It sounds too simple, doesn't it? It's been said before, and you're going to hear it again:

However nervous, unhappy, or fed up you're feeling, stick a smile on your face and make those learners think there's nowhere else you'd rather be than there in that classroom with that particular class and teaching that particular topic.

6. Smile

There's an old song that tells you to smile even though your heart is breaking. This can be very good advice for when you're in the classroom. A smile says you're feeling relaxed. It says you're feeling confident. It says you're happy to be there. It also says, *'I like you and I like my job'*. These are good messages. Smiling can even make you feel more confident. One reason for this is the tendency we humans have to mirror the expressions or body language of those we're communicating with. So when you smile at learners, you're likely to find some of them smiling back. And that can be a real confidence booster.

7. Look-a-like

Behave as though you like your learners. Perhaps you do – in which case this is easy. Or perhaps they cause you problems and you don't look forward to teaching them. That's when this strategy can seem difficult. But it's important to remember that the teacher–learner relationship is crucial to learners' motivation. They need to believe that you have a positive regard for them. There may sometimes be a learner or learners whom you find difficult to like. This can't be helped. What's important is that you never show it. You can certainly show that you dislike some of their behaviours; but for learners themselves you should always show a positive regard – for all of them equally.

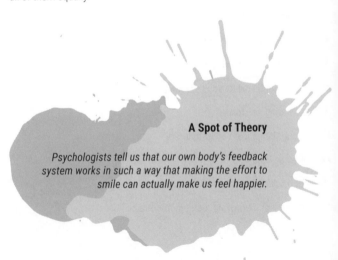

A Spot of Theory

Psychologists tell us that our own body's feedback system works in such a way that making the effort to smile can actually make us feel happier.

Picture this:

The teacher stands in front of the class. The class is making a lot of noise. The teacher is frowning. She claps her hands twice and shouts at them to be quiet. They keep making a noise. She scowls at them. She shouts more loudly. She singles out a table near the front and shouts at them to be quiet.

" *I'm sick and tired of you lot!*

Then she shouts at the class,

" *I'm sick and tired of trying to make myself heard over your noise.*

She stands there a bit longer.

" *I'M STILL WAITING!*

The noise continues.

" *WELL, THAT'S YOUR LOOK OUT!*

She stamps her foot.

" *I can wait here all day! I don't care if you don't learn anything! If you're all too stupid to bother, why should I care?*

And she goes and sits down at her table. The noise continues …

Now picture this:

The teacher stands in front of the class. The class is making a lot of noise. The teacher looks relaxed and is smiling. She claps her hands twice and raises them in the air. She looks around the class, smiling. When she catches a learner's eye she puts a finger to her lips. Then she walks over to a table near the front, still smiling.

" *Everybody alright?*

The learners at that table quieten down and nod and say yes. She goes to the next table and does the same thing. The room is getting quieter now. Addressing the whole class she says,

" *Well now! Good to see you all. And good to hear you've all got so much energy today, because we've got a lot of interesting work to do. So let's make a start.*

The class has quietened down.

Question:

⚫ Which teacher will now be feeling stronger and more confident?

Strategy: Breathing and mindfulness

We've already noted that teaching is a little like being on the stage – and can sometimes seem as nerve-wracking. Actors have all sorts of strategies for coping with nerves or stress before a performance. Some of these, such as breathing exercises or techniques to gather and calm the thoughts, can be very useful to teachers, too. Here are two you can try:

8. Breathe stress away

Set your weight evenly on both feet and be aware of the contact between the soles of your feet and the floor. Breathe in, and at the same time feel your tummy expand. Then breathe out slowly as though you are blowing a feather, at the same time feeling your tummy draw in. Do this five or six times. It ensures you get plenty of oxygen to your brain so that you can think clearly; and it prevents you from hyperventilating, which can make you feel anxious and muddled. This is a calming exercise you can even do in the classroom itself, if necessary, without anyone noticing.

9. Mindfulness

A lot has been written recently about mindfulness – so it's possible you're already familiar with the concept. Being mindful is about focusing your mind on the moment, rather than allowing it to go galloping off in all directions pursuing your anxieties and worries. When you're mid-lesson and your thoughts are flying here, there and everywhere – *'What if this goes wrong? What if that group starts playing up now? What if I forget what I'm supposed to be saying? I've got another class to teach and I haven't planned my lesson yet. I don't think this class likes me...'* – bring yourself back to the moment. Concentrate on what's happening here and now. Focus on what's actually happening and give it your entire attention. It won't make the worries and anxieties go away, but it will allow you to observe and – for now – ignore them, until the appropriate time comes to do something about them.

A Spot of Theory

Academics and researchers Mark Williams and Danny Penman in their book, Mindfulness *(2011, Piatkus, p 5), cite scientific studies which have shown how* 'mindfulness positively affects the brain patterns underlying day-to-day anxiety, stress, depression and irritability so that when they arise they dissolve away again more easily.'

This is what one teacher has to say:

" *When I started out I was having real trouble with the class. I was beginning to dread going in. I had this feeling of doom, as though one of these days it was all going to go so badly wrong that I'd probably end up running out of there crying. And it must have showed, because in the end my mentor sat me down and asked me whether I was having trouble with that class. And it was such a relief to tell her, because they'd always behaved when she was in there, observing. But she said she knew they could be difficult because others teachers had said so. And she said she would give me some tips on how to calm myself down and go in there feeling more confident. She said that if I felt more confident, I would look more confident; and if the class started to see me looking confident they wouldn't regard me as such an easy target and they'd be less likely to play up. And she was right! She gave me this breathing exercise to do, to help me slow down my breathing before I go into the classroom. It's helped such a lot. It seems to clear the panic out of my head so that I can think more clearly and calmly. It helps me keep everything in proportion. I've even used it in the middle of class when I'm standing by the board. No one can tell. But I can! It makes such a difference. It really helps me to concentrate and keep alert in the here and now. It's made a real difference to my teaching.*

Strategy: Making the most of your position

10. Your advantage

You may feel anxious when you face a difficult class. You may believe that the learners will somehow know that you are inexperienced or nervous. You may feel that, because there's only one of you and many of them, the dice are loaded against you and that you'll never be able to gain their attention or their respect. If you do feel like this, what you may be forgetting is that your role as the teacher gives you an automatic advantage. You're positioned in the place where the figure of authority is expected to be. You get to start the lesson and bring it to a close. You get to announce the topic. By the time learners have been in the system for a year or two, most of them have been conditioned to see the person at the front as the one in charge. It may not always feel that way to you, but nevertheless it's important to keep it in mind. In terms of who's controlling the classroom, you do start from a position of advantage. It's then up to you to build on it.

A very useful way of seeing how this looks in action is to arrange to have one of your teaching sessions (or part of one) video recorded. The camera should be firmly on you, of course. As soon as you can – the same day if possible – watch it through on your own and ask yourself the following questions:

✳ Do I look more confident than I was feeling? (The answer to this is usually a surprising YES!)

✳ Am I positioning myself in the best place to gain everyone's attention?

✳ Am I projecting my voice sufficiently to be heard by everyone (without actually shouting)?

✳ Does my voice convey enthusiasm and energy and enjoyment?

✳ What is my body language saying to the class? Is it saying, *'I'm enjoying this!'* Or is it saying, *'I'd rather be anywhere else but here'*?

✳ Am I moving around, occupying the room as the role of teacher entitles me to?

✳ Where am I looking? Am I focusing more on one side of the room or one group than another?

✳ Am I smiling – at least some of the time?

✳ Am I doing all the talking or am I also listening with interest to what learners say?

✳ What have I learnt from watching this and what – if anything – am I going to change about the way I present myself to a class?

If you're unable to organise a video recording, you could ask your mentor or a colleague to sit in for half an hour and make notes of what they see. Or you could rely on your memory. But there is no confidence boost quite so effective as seeing yourself on video and being able to say, *'I was feeling really nervous there, but I just don't look it at all!'*

Strategy: Keeping it all in perspective

11. Nothing personal

The teacher may be a handy target for disruptive behaviour, but in most cases, as we've seen, they're a target *only because they are the teacher*. In that sense, it's very rarely personal. If you take learners' disruptive behaviour personally you won't be able to think clearly and dispassionately about what strategies are needed to address it; and you won't bother trying to discover the real reasons behind the behaviour. This means you'll be less likely to succeed in getting the learner back on board and engaged with their learning.

So always remember this:

The learner who is making things difficult is unlikely to have anything against you personally.

Much disruptive behaviour arises from learner's previous negative experiences or their low expectations of authority figures, the learning process, or both. They may assume they'll find you hostile or dismissive because that's what their prior experiences have taught them to expect. They think they're going to find your lessons boring because they've always been bored in class before. This may drive them to behave in a disengaged or disruptive way. It's not about you. Their behaviour is something which needs to be treated as a professional challenge, not as a personal one.

Read this scenario and:

1. Decide what you think is the reason behind the learner's disruptive behaviour. You'll see a list of possible reasons. Tick the one you think is most likely.

2. Consider what, in your view, would be appropriate 'consequences' for Ella's behaviour.

The teacher is trying to settle the class. Ella won't stop talking. When the teacher asks her to be quiet, Ella tosses her head and says: *'Why should I?'* The teacher explains why. Ella holds up a hand, palm outwards, and says, *'I'm not listening, so you might as well stop talking'*. The teacher tells Ella that there will be consequences for her rude behaviour, but that he's now going to continue the lesson. Ella, however, continues with attempts to disrupt everything. She sniggers and makes audible comments about what the teacher is wearing. The teacher ignores her. He's already made sure the whole class has heard him warn her there'd be consequences, so they know she's not simply going to get away with it. Ella, frustrated at getting no reaction, asks if she can go to the toilet. The teacher allows her to leave the room. The lesson continues peacefully – until she comes back in.

What's the likely reason for Ella's behaviour? Is it because:

* Ella is having trouble at home?
* She left home without breakfast and is grumpy with hunger?
* She's worried about her grandma?
* She's fallen out with her boyfriend/girlfriend?
* Her best friend isn't speaking to her?
* She has a personal dislike of the teacher?
* She's lost her phone and is scared of getting into trouble over it at home?
* She's afraid she won't be able to do the work so she's avoiding joining in?
* She wants the other learners to think she's tough?

Answer

☑ It could be absolutely any of them! But if the teacher takes it personally he'll be unlikely to discover the actual cause.

If you only try one thing from this chapter, try this*

Checklist

Use this to keep a record of what worked well for you and what didn't. A strategy that works with one class may not work so well with another. Keeping a checklist helps you to work out what factors or learner characteristics call for one approach rather than another. There's a line at the bottom for you to add your own most frequently used strategy, if it's not already included in the list.

Strategy	Tried it with...	On (date)	It worked	It didn't work	Worth trying again?
1. Laugh and the world laughs with you...					
2. They who laugh first...					
3. The mask					
4. Respond, don't react					
5. Feel the fear					
6. Smile					
7. Look-a-like*					
8. Breathe stress away					
9. Mindfulness					
10. Your advantage					
11. Nothing personal					
Your own strategy?					

Further reading

If you'd like to read more about some of the theories mentioned in this book, or to find out more about the strategies and how they have been arrived at or applied in practice, here is a list of texts which are readily available, in electronic format or as hard copy.

Bates, B (2015) *Learning Theories Simplified: … And How to Apply Them to Teaching.* London: Sage.

Beattie, G (2016) *Rethinking Body Language: How Hand Movements Reveal Hidden Thoughts*. Hove: Psychology Press

Bruhlmeier, A (2010) *Head, Heart and Hand: Education in the Spirit of Pestalozzi.* Cambridge: Open Book Publishers.

Dix, P (2010)*The Essential Guide to Taking Care of Behaviour: Practical Skills for Teachers.* Harlow: Pearson/Longman.

Dweck, C (2012) *Mindset: How You Can Fulfil Your Potential.* London: Robinson.

Gershon, M (2016) *How to Develop Growth Mindsets in the Classroom.* Createspace Independent Publishing Platform.

Lever, C (2011) *Understanding Challenging Behaviour in Inclusive Classrooms.* Abingdon-on-Thames: Routledge

Maslow, A (2013) *A Theory of Human Motivation (editor David Webb).* CreateSpace Independent Publishing Platform.

Plevin, R (2016) *Take Control of the Noisy Class*. Camarthen: Crown House.

Rogers, B (2006) *Cracking the Hard Class.* London: Paul Chapman Publishing.

Rogers, B (2015) *Classroom Behaviour (4th edn).* London: Sage.

Rutledge, T (2012) *Embracing Fear: How to Turn What Scares Us into our Greatest Gift.* London: HarperOne.

Sunderland, M (2015) *Conversations That Matter: Talking with Children and Teenagers in Ways That Help.* Franklin, US: Worth Publishing.

Wallace, I and Kirkman, L (2014) *Talk-Less Teaching: Practice, Participation and Progress*. Camarthen: Crown House.

Wallace, S (2014) When You're Smiling: Exploring How Teachers Motivate and Engage Learners in the Further Education Sector. *Journal of Further and Higher Education*, 38(3): 346–60.

Williams, M and Penman, D (2011) *Mindfulness: A Practical Guide to Finding Peace in a Frantic World*. London: Piatkus.

Wolstenholme, K (2003) *Kinaesthetic Learning Activities in the Primary School.* Birmingham: Birmingham Advisory and Support Service.

CRITICAL PUBLISHING

Register with Critical Publishing to:

- be the first to know about forthcoming titles;
- find out more about our new Getting it Right in a Week series;
- sign up for our regular newsletter for special offers, discount codes and more.

Visit our website at:

www.criticalpublishing.com